Praise for *Tangible Grace*

Tangible Grace is an essential, life-saving read for all religious leaders, communities, parents, and scholars who care about the well-being of teens. Evelyn L. Parker tackles a too-often-neglected critical issue in religious life—gender-based and intimate partner violence among teenagers. This book stuns with powerful questions such as: How is the faith and spirituality of a teenager shaped when [their] body hurts during Sunday worship—a site of Christian faith formation—from slaps and punches administered just hours before? With deeply moving narratives, Parker makes readers aware of the problem of violence in teenage romantic relationships, including same-gender teen partners, and offers practical guidance for how to teach, preach to, worship with, pastorally care for, and advocate on behalf of teens. Combining knowledge from her long history of working with and on behalf of young people with insightful wisdom from other leading practical theologians, Parker challenges us to see teenage bodies as tangible manifestations of God's grace and provokes us toward emancipatory pedagogies that stand against gender-based violence. As a religious educator and practical theologian, I see *Tangible Grace* as the critical and creative book I've been missing in my courses.

> **Rachelle R. Green**, assistant professor of practical
> theology and education, Fordham University

Tangible Grace by Evelyn L. Parker addresses teen dating violence through a theological lens, emphasizing tangible grace and using ministerial practices like teaching, preaching, and pastoral care to prevent and intervene. It highlights the importance of addressing implicit gender-based violence in religious and educational settings. Parker offers a provocative understanding of grace that she describes as tangible grace. The book explores ministry interventions for addressing teen dating violence, emphasizing the theological concept of tangible grace as God's gift of the human body.

Weaving science, theological spirituality, and storytelling, womanist scholar Evelyn Parker unmasks the unthinkable, undiscussed, unseen realities of gender-based violence in adolescent relationships. With an overwhelmingly gentle tone and radically inclusive approach, Parker offers this well-researched, beautifully written, and cutting-edge volume to those intentionally nurturing adolescents, those searching for a resource to teach/preach a holistic approach to sexuality, and those needing a practical powerful pathway back to divine love when tangible grace has been distorted.

Alison Gise Johnson, womanist scholar and associate professor of philosophy, Claflin University

Tangible Grace is a powerful text that not only lays bare the problem of teen dating violence but also offers approaches through teaching, liturgy and worship, pastoral care, preaching, and advocacy to aid in both prevention and intervention. As a womanist Christian educator and practical theologian, former youth minister and youth institute director, someone who experienced teen dating violence, and a mother of two boys, I find this text to be not only a must-read but a must-implement and must-act. Educators, practitioners, laypersons, parents, and grandparents: we all need to heed Parker's words and take this reality seriously by implementing the approaches she suggests. When we fail to act, we enable and aid in the tormenting of teens' tangible grace. The lives and well-being of our youth are at stake.

Lakisha R. Lockhart, assistant professor of Christian education, Union Presbyterian Seminary, and author of *Doing Theological Double Dutch: A Womanist Pedagogy of Play*

Evelyn L. Parker highlights the prevalence of intimate partner violence among teenagers and the importance of awareness and intervention and suggests using religious teachings, pastoral care, and advocacy to prevent and address teen dating violence. Parker's teaching strategies include integrating gender-based violence education into human sexuality courses and using emancipatory pedagogy and subversive teaching of holy scriptures to address systemic issues of patriarchy and power contributing to gender-based violence. The book invites us to see the role teaching plays in addressing gender-based violence. We are also given tools to combat teen violence, such as the use of implicit curriculum and religious teachings.

Carmichael Crutchfield, vice president of Academic Affairs and academic dean; Clara Scott Chair of Church and Ministry; professor of Christian education, spiritual formation, and youth ministry, Memphis Theological Seminary, and General Secretary of the Department of Christian Education and Formation, Christian Methodist Episcopal Church

Evelyn L. Parker's *Tangible Grace: Ministry Interventions for Teen Dating Violence* is an essential resource for addressing the pressing issue of teen dating violence in our communities. Through theological insight and practical strategies, Parker empowers ministry leaders to foster healing and transformation. This book is a profound guide for creating safe spaces that affirm the dignity and worth of every teenager.

Latricia Edwards Scriven, pastor and author of When Jesus Laughs

This is a book of collective wisdom from the various branches of practical theology. Parker places insight, theory, and best practices in conversation with each other to help young people whose tangible grace has been tormented. The topics discussed and Parker's approach make this text essential reading for those involved in the spiritual formation of young people.

Annie Lockhart-Gilroy, associate professor of Christian education and practical theology and director of the Doctor of Ministry Program, Phillips Theological Seminary, and author of *Nurturing the Sanctified Imagination of Urban Youth*

As a pioneering womanist practical theologian, Evelyn Parker has created an invaluable resource for ministry practitioners with her groundbreaking work, *Tangible Grace: Ministry Interventions for Teen Dating Violence*. Guided by a profound commitment to intersectional understanding—deeply attentive to race, class, gender, and sexual identity—her book offers a comprehensive approach to youth ministry that centers on reverential love, bodily dignity, and holistic healing. Drawing from a rich tapestry of personal sacred memories, scholarly research, and compelling narratives, Parker illuminates the critical issue of gender-based violence among teenagers in the United States. Her work is distinctively rooted in a careful consideration of the lived religious beliefs of girls and young-adult women, providing a nuanced and deeply empathetic exploration of their experiences. What sets this volume apart is its expansive vision of ministerial responsibility. Parker persuasively argues that every aspect of ministry—from preaching to pastoral care, from Christian education to liturgical planning—carries a unique opportunity and obligation to create safe spaces for young people. She empowers ministry leaders to recognize their collective role in protecting and nurturing youth, and for endowing them with an abiding sense of their own agency. Central to Parker's approach is the powerful theological assertion that every body is an enfleshment of God's grace, and as such, God wills the complete wholeness, healing, and flourishing of young people. By emphasizing self-love, respect, and intentional care, she provides a framework for ministry that goes beyond traditional models, offering a profound reimagining of youth spiritual support. This book is essential reading for anyone committed to working with youth or desiring to make their ministries genuinely relevant to young people's lived experiences. Parker has gifted the faith community with a compassionate, scholarly, and deeply practical guide that has the potential to transform how we approach youth ministry. I recommend this book for pastors, youth ministers, educators, counselors, and anyone passionate about supporting and empowering young people in their faith journey.

Neichelle R. Guidry, dean of Sisters Chapel and director of the WISDOM Center, Spelman College

Evelyn L. Parker places the uncomfortable topic of teen dating violence on the table and navigates us through its complex layers like only a womanist practical theologian can. This wise and care-filled guide offers best practices for religious leaders searching for approaches to prevent and intervene in teen dating violence. This is a ministry resource every person called to care for youth ought to read.

Gina A. S. Robinson, program officer of Racial Justice and Diversity in Unity, Wayfarer Foundation

Sometimes the conversations that should happen in faith communities are the very ones that seem absent or even off-limits. In *Tangible Grace*, Evelyn L. Parker leans into her committed vocation of liberative practical theological scholarship by breaking open a needed conversation about teen dating violence—a type of traumatic experience that impacts one in every twelve high school teens but tends to be easily overlooked in church curricula. Parker makes an inspiring and compelling theological case for congregations to incorporate intentional formation and care related to the matter while providing practical guides and pathways forward. *Tangible Grace* can fit well in a course on youth ministry or pastoral care, but it can also be a helpful book for church staff members and volunteers to read together.

Montague R. Williams, professor of church, culture, and society, Point Loma Nazarene University, and author of *Church in Color: Youth Ministry, Race, and the Theology of Martin Luther King Jr.*

TANGIBLE
GRACE

TANGIBLE GRACE

Ministry Interventions for Teen Dating Violence

EVELYN L. PARKER

Fortress Press
Minneapolis

TANGIBLE GRACE
Ministry Interventions for Teen Dating Violence

30 29 28 27 26 25   1 2 3 4 5 6 7 8 9

All Scripture quotations, unless otherwise indicated, are from the New Revised Standard Version Bible, copyright © 1989 National Council of the Churches of Christ in the United States of America. Used by permission. All rights reserved worldwide.

Sacred Awakening: Lessons on the Path, Poems, Essay and Illustrations published by permission of Christopher John Ahrends.

Service of Hope for Teen Victims of Dating Violence adapted from The United Methodist Book of Worship and *The Formation of a People: Christian Education and the African American Church* by Carmichael D. Crutchfield. Copyright © 2020 by Judson Press. Used by permission of Judson Press.

"O Living Breath of God" hymn, text: Osvaldo Catena, 1920–1986; tr. Gerhard M. Cartford, 1923–2016 Tr. © 1998 Augsburg Fortress. Reproduced by permission.

"Prayer after the Laying on of Hands" adapted from *The United Methodist Book of Worship*, 621 © 1992 The United Methodist Publishing House. Used by permission. All rights reserved.

Library of Congress Control Number: 2024950042 (print)

Cover design: Ashley Muehlbauer
Cover illustration: Exploding powder with white background captured with high speed sync, from Xvision/Getty Images

Print ISBN: 979-8-8898-3331-4
eBook ISBN: 979-8-8898-3332-1

To all the many teenagers who have
suffered from gender-based violence.

Contents

Acknowledgments

This book is part of a slow march toward justice for teenagers who have experienced or are at risk of experiencing dating violence. The book actually started January 18–20, 2018, at the Center for Youth Ministry Training at Austin Presbyterian Theological Seminary in Austin, Texas, when I gave a lecture titled "#MeToo Tweets the Pastor" and taught two workshops titled #MeToo: Pastors Preaching and Teaching Prevention of Teen Dating Violence. It was the response of youth ministers that gave me the impetus to continue the journey. When I stepped off the stage, women and men lined up on opposite sides of the lecture hall to thank me one by one for discussing the sensitive issue of dating violence, to share their stories of date rape, and to ask for advice on how to deal with similar issues in their youth groups. Their responses helped launch my crusade for practical theological approaches for preventing and intervening in teen dating violence.

Since then, the list of people and resource providers to acknowledge is long, and I am sure I will forget to name some of them. So please accept my apology at the onset of these words of thanks if I failed to acknowledge you. Your support in bringing this book to completion is deeply appreciated.

Research for *Tangible Grace* required several financial resources. The Southern Methodist University Sam Taylor Fellowship funded my initial research on "#MeToo Tweets the Pastor." The J. William Fulbright Scholar Award 2019–2020 supported my research in South Africa, primarily in Cape

Town and other regions of the Western Cape province. The Perkins School of Theology Scholarly Outreach Award provided funding for the research in the United States as well as for writing and analyzing interview transcriptions.

Equally important to financial support were the many friends and colleagues who connected me to religious leaders, youth leaders, and parents as I sought interviews with people concerned about teen dating violence. Many among this wonderful group also were my conversation partners. The US Consulate Office in Cape Town was very supportive of my research. I am deeply grateful to Professor Sarojini Nadar, director and research chair of the Desmond Tutu Centre for Religion and Social Justice at the University of the Western Cape. Professor Nadar, the Tutu Centre scholars, lecturers, staff, and students provided my academic home base while in South Africa. The Tutu Centre and the University of the Western Cape Department of Religion provided opportunities to present my research to the university community.

I'm also grateful to Dr. John Klaasen and the University of the Western Cape Department of Religion for providing me an office and opportunities to meet and get to know students. Ms. Claudene Sebolai, a graduate student and lecturer, provided outstanding support as my research assistant and interlocutor. The South African Faith and Family Institute— Elizabeth Petersen, director, and Lynn-Joy Isaacs and Katie Roman, staff members—invited me to join them in teaching at gender-based-violence workshops, which connected me to potential interviewees. Their connections with the greater Cape Town communities were invaluable. I'm also thankful for conversations about teen dating violence with Stacey Riley, director of the Gulf Coast Center for Nonviolence in Biloxi, Mississippi, and members of her staff who work with community schools.

I'm deeply appreciative to Miranda Pillay, Extraordinary Professor at the University of the Western Cape, affiliated with the Desmond Tutu Centre for Religion and Social Justice. Professor Pillay was my constant conversation partner about the context of my South African interviewees and the theoretical ideas in my manuscript.

Among the audiences that heard some of my research were students and faculty at the College of Transfiguration Makhanda in Grahamstown in the Eastern Cape province, an Anglican theological institution. I am very grateful to the Rev. Dr. Vicentia Kgabe, who as rector invited me to lecture in 2019. Also, parts of this book's introduction come from my Sprunt Lecture on May 4, 2020, at Union Presbyterian Theological Seminary. I am very grateful to President Brian K. Blount for the invitation and the engagement of my ideas with alums, students, and faculty. Students and faculty at Cliff College, United Kingdom, heard parts of my theoretical framework for the book. And, last but not least, my students at Garrett-Evangelical Theological Seminary in Evanston, Illinois, heard bits and pieces of my ethnographic methodology.

My editor extraordinaire, Ulrike Guthrie, edited the first draft of my manuscript. Ulrike has a wonderful way of pushing me to clarify my thoughts and ideas while affirming my storytelling. She helped me prepare the manuscript for the proposal phase.

My editor with Fortress Press, Yvonne D. Hawkins, has been invaluable for honing my ideas and words into the book that I am proud to own. She affirmed and pushed me each step of the process for this book to be produced. I am so thankful for her editorial brilliance.

I am grateful to my mother, Geraldine F. Parker, for affirming my calling as a teacher and scholar who continues to write and publish even though retired. I am also deeply grateful to my partner, James F. Armstrong, who made space and time for me to write uninterrupted as well as provided opportunities for rest and recreation. You are generous beyond words.

Most importantly, this book would not have been possible had I not been blessed with the stories of my interviewees in Cape Town, Western Cape province, South Africa, and in the United States. You shared stories with me interview after interview, over tea and cookies before the Covid pandemic, and via Zoom and telephone during the quarantine period of the pandemic. Your commitment to the thriving of young people showed in your experiences with them and their families. I am eternally grateful for your contributions to this book.

Introduction

We have so much in common, she said. We are both biracial and have experienced some of the same types of racism. He is a senior, and I am a sophomore. I love the fact that he is a football star. Recently, he became possessive, telling me what I could and could not wear, what I could and could not do. He hit me a couple of times. He emotionally and physically abused me. I was so depressed I started back cutting. I feel God is selfish for not allowing me to be happy. All I want is to be happy with a boyfriend like me.

—A High School Student

The account above is a true story of a cisgender female teenage student whom I knew while serving as counselor for a youth theological program in Texas. Notice the physical and psychological abuse, the controlling behavior the student describes. These are all primary indicators of intimate partner violence as defined by the Centers for Disease Control and Prevention (CDC). And a teenager was experiencing it.

Al Miles, hospital chaplain and advocate for women who have experienced violence, highlights issues of denial about teen dating violence.[1] Miles notes that many teenagers believe that hitting, slapping, and similar behavior are acceptable, so they do not constitute dating violence. Pastoral theologians also note that some clergy and parents likewise find it hard to conceive of this type of behavior as violence in teenage or youth romantic relationships. Some clergy and parents believe teens are exhibiting playful behavior, which they understand to be normal for middle and high school students. There is a thin line between teenage play and the potential for teenage abusive practices. However, the actions that the student above describes exhibit manifestations or signs of gender-based violence among teenagers or youth. The problem exists among this age demographic, just as gender-based and intimate-partner violence exist among older cohorts.

My goal is to make readers aware of the problem of violence in teenage romantic relationships, including same-gender-loving teen partners, if you do not already realize how rampant it is, or to build on your awareness of the problem if you are familiar with it. I want to theologically consider this egregious sin through the idea of *tangible grace*. I define *tangible grace* as God's gracious, material gift of the touchable, physiological body. A theological examination of the harm that violence among intimate teenage partners brings on their bodies renders their tangible grace *tormented*. A youth involved in a violent, intimate relationship is someone who painfully suffers physically, mentally, and spiritually even as their teenage bodies are gifts of God's grace.

Using best practices obtained from various religious leaders, this book offers approaches that religious leaders can use to prevent and intervene in teen dating violence, primarily through their relationships with teens in the context of their religious communities, using various ministerial practices. This book addresses the prevention and intervention of teen dating violence through the five ministry contexts of teaching, preaching and sacred rhetoric, liturgy and worship, pastoral care, and advocacy.

Please note that I use the terms *teenagers* and *youth* interchangeably.[2] These terms refer to people ages eleven to eighteen, the ages of young people who are ordinarily in junior high and high school in the United States. The CDC targets eleven- to twenty-four-year-olds in their publications on prevention of teen dating violence and indicates instances of violence occurring among teens as young as eleven years old.[3] I include this age group up through high school.

I also use the terms *teen dating violence* and *gender-based violence*, given that they are noted by the CDC. *Gender-based violence* is an umbrella term for violence based on what is considered as an inferior gender in power-driven relationships. When gender-based violence occurrs among eleven- to eighteen-year-olds, I use the term *teen dating violence.*

Meanwhile, I developed the concept of tangible grace in 2010 as a theological framework for thinking about the human body and our Christian practice of honoring the gift of the human body through ways that include exercise, resting, and adorning the body.[4] I define the human body itself as tangible grace. The human body is God's creative design of billions of cells that are orchestrated to create us—as unique individuals. God gave us our bodies for our delight and enjoyment, and the delight and enjoyment of others, as well as for God's own delight. God's love becomes tangible, touchable, and embodied through our bodies.[5] While tangible grace signifies God's unmerited gift of the human body, this concept can be understood more clearly if we first reflect on the meaning of *grace* that is being modified in the term *tangible grace.*

To do this, I draw on the wisdom of theologian Serene Jones in *Call It Grace: Finding Meaning in a Fractured World.* Jones uses stories from various milestones in her life—what she calls *stations*—to develop a theology that shaped who she was as she turned sixty and beyond. The book is Jones's theological life story,[6] with a central theme of grace, which she conceptualizes in six core beliefs. The first two core beliefs are

1. "*God is mystery.*" Hence we can never know completely who and what God "is." Yet, she declares, "I actually believe infinitely and with certainty that the mystery we cannot know is loving, indeed, it is Love, and that in this Love we find our true existence."

2. *"This infinite mystery is our creator, sustainer, and ulti-
    mately, our consummator, our beginning, our middle,
    and our end."* Divine Love, she argues, "is the source of
    the universe [all things past, present, and future] . . . the
    force that sparked us into existence and baffles us all while
    we exist, the current of love and joy and beauty that runs
    through the human experience. . . . The world [is] God's
    ever-sustained creation and us as God's creatures. Exis-
    tence, in its entirety, from beginning to end, is dependent
    upon and always connected to and inspired by the source
    from which it flows, God. . . . All life flows into being out
    of one source, Divine Love, and it is forever deeply related
    and responsive to that love. That love defines, holds, and
    promises to be present to the lives that God calls into
    being. That eternally present love is, most simply stated,
    my definition of *grace*."[7]

The underlying premise is that Divine Love is grace. I argue
that grace understood in this manner is compatible with the
human body as grace—as Divine Love—that is touchable or
tangible. The human body is a manifestation of God's Divine
Love, God's grace. A teenager or youth is a manifestation of
Divine Love because this grace is ageless. The somatic divine
gift of the human body is beautifully designed in a multiplicity
of ways. Yet, we categorize human bodies as deviant, disabled,
normal, or abnormal.[8] Human bodies we deem to be abnormal were created within the mysterious realm of perfection
through God's Divine Love, *grace*.

Likewise, we assign gender, race, and sexuality to our tangible grace. We say that we or others are cisgender male, cisgender female, binary, nonbinary, or transgender. Regardless of
the labels we assign, our bodies are tangible grace.

Adolescence is that crucial developmental stage in the
human life cycle at which teenagers question their identity
in a multiplicity of ways that can include their race, gender,
and sexual orientation. Teens question their racial or ethnic

identity when they ask: Who am I with my black or brown skin? Who am I when my friends call me red bone or yellow bone? Who am I when adults call me paper-bag brown or boot black? Who am I with my kinky red hair, blue eyes, and yellow skin tone? The quest for racial or ethnic identity is complex for a teenager who might not have experienced affirmation that their yellow, brown, or chocolate skin tone, their kinky or straight hair texture, or their nose, lips, and hips are perfect creations of God.

Likewise, teens question their identity as gendered persons. Some teens choose to identify their gender according to how they were classified at birth, which almost inevitably means they call themselves a cisgender female or a cisgender male. To identify oneself as cisgender moves away from binary assumptions about the social construct of gender. Hence, teenagers who take authority to identify their gender and sexuality on their own terms are affirming the normalcy of their tangible grace. Teenagers who have a sense of their identity as racialized, gendered, and sexualized bodies are affirming their creation within the mysterious realm of perfection through tangible grace.

As Jones states, "Jesus Christ stands as the truest and most vivid and profound human manifestation" of Divine Love.[9] Yes. Jesus also stands as the truest and most vivid manifestation of what it means to have a body. Jesus was Divine Love enfleshed. The human Jesus had bodily functions like you and me. He ate food, drank beverages, expelled bodily wastes and fluids; he slept, walked, and talked. He had emotions and was intellectually astute. That is what the incarnation means: that Divine Love—God—took on human flesh. Like Jesus, we are touchable, human love. Like Jesus, we—and specifically teenagers—are tangible grace.

Our humanity, created in God's goodness, has the capacity to love as God loves. We love different groups of people for different reasons, people who include friends, partners, wives, and husbands. Our love for another is an aspect of our spirituality. The touchable human body as tangible grace helps us think about touching God's divine love through our bodies. Being human requires our own and others' touching of our bodies, the touching of tangible grace. "The boundary of skin that our bodies place between us can be bridged through the touch of another."[10] Stephanie Paulsell, professor of the practice of Christian studies at Harvard Divinity School, reminds us of the importance of touching by recounting the story of a young adult in need of touch while away from home, family, and friends. She writes:

> A student living alone in Italy for a year reports that she attended mass every evening in the small town where she lived, to worship God not only through word and sacrament but through touch. Living alone, she often went all day without feeling a human touch. The ritual movement of passing the peace was the high point of the service for her, because it provided a safe space to touch and be touched by other people—even people whom she did not know.[11]

A child learns appropriate touch from a loving parent, who bathes her body, wipes her nose, and dries her tears. The teenager remembers love through the touch of a parent as she moves into relationships with friends. During their first dance or first kiss, teens recall appropriate touch by a loving parent or trusted friend. Those good experiences remind them to be aware also of inappropriate touch by an adult or anyone who breaches the boundaries of appropriate touch, even touching that hurts their body. When a teenager is hurt by inappropriate touch, the harm that results is tormenting to the tangible grace that is their body. There are consequences of bad or abusive touching that torments the teenaged body. Aspects of bad touch are explored in chapter 4. For now, let us consider tangible grace's gift of intimate touching.

Torment and Tangible Grace

Tangible grace is the gift of the human body. Our bodies, with all their biological and psychological systems, are a tangible gift—a gift we can experience with our senses. Our bodies are a material manifestation of God's divine gift. Our flesh is diverse, visible in many hues, sizes and shapes, and verbal accents. Yet, we are all made in the same goodness and likeness of God—the *imago Dei.* Our bodies were "knit together in [our] mother's womb" (Ps 139:13) by the power of God's love working in the physiological development of our members.

God created our physical bodies with the sense of touch. While we are endowed with the capacity to perceive the world through the senses of sight, smell, hearing, and taste, the sense of touch is skin-to-skin perception of the world. There are rare diseases that impair our ability to feel with our skin, such as forms of congenital insensitivity to pain. However, touching others or being touched by others is an aspect of our human development that begins at birth and is evaluated during the first ninety days of life.[12] We learn from infancy what is good touch and what is bad, what heals and what hurts. However, a desperate need for love and intimacy, specifically among teenagers, can distort knowing what good touch is. Teenagers need guidance on what is good touch in all their relationships, especially romantic or dating relationships.

Tangible grace is tormented by distortions of good touch in teen dating relationships. Consider the good touch of love and intimacy that becomes distorted over time. Imagine for a moment the young love that sparks between two first-year high school students who meet and touch during orientation, in the gym, in the cafeteria, or in class. A handshake, mistakenly bumping arms while reaching for a glass, and even a tap on the shoulder to alert someone that they dropped a pen are possible ways that touching can lead to an intimate relationship. As two students develop their loving relationship, first with conversation, then dating, and then a commitment to "going steady," their touch becomes directed toward pleasing and pleasuring each other through kissing, hugging, and possibly sexual foreplay and intercourse. All these activities are expressions of love and intimacy through good touch.

However, when a partner in a teen dating relationship begins to shove, pinch, or exhibit other forms of abusive physical behavior, tangible grace is distorted, and touching hurts. There is a need for pastoral care and counseling when a teen believes his partner is expressing love and affection when the partner exhibits physically violent behavior. Susan Sanders, professor emeritus of history and political science and director of the Center for Religion and Public Discourse at Saint Xavier University in Chicago, argues against misinterpreting actions of a teen shoving or punching their partner as love or concern.[13] Some teen partners do not view such behavior as abusive or feel they inadvertently provoked the behavior. Sanders surveyed young teenage women about girls who persist in physically abusive relationships. They were asked to respond to statements that included: "I wouldn't keep dating a boyfriend who kicks me (77.7% agreed and about 13% disagreed); If a boyfriend threw something at me while we were dating, I would think it no big deal (83.7% disagreed and 11.5% neither agreed or disagreed, 4.8% agreed)."[14] "Of the 386 survey respondents who said they had dated within a year of the administration of the survey, 5.7 percent reported that they had experienced physical abuse."[15] When responding to questions about being kicked, punched, pulled by the hair, shoved, held down by the shoulders, bruised or bitten, wrestled with roughly, driven fast to scare, and being physically stopped, 34 percent had experienced one or more behaviors at least once.[16]

While touching that hurts implies physical hurting of a teen in an abusive dating relationship, touching that hurts also includes the emotional hurt caused by abusive dating relationships. There are several sets of behaviors indicative of emotional abuse. Controlling and isolating abusive actions put the teen in a submissive position and diminish their autonomy and personal authority, manifest mistrust, and involve or suggest stalking.[17] These signs are usually present at the onset of a violent dating relationship.[18] Disrespectful behavior is a second set of abusive behaviors that hurt. Sanders focuses on three types among a long list of disrespectful behaviors in her research: "the experience of being made to wait for one's boyfriend; the experience of a boyfriend's making fun of his dating partner or her family or friends; and being shouted or sworn at."[19] While Sanders's research focuses on teenage girls abused by teenage boys her findings can be applied to same-gender-loving teenagers. In both situations, physical or emotional abuse in teen dating relationships, pastoral care and counseling can be preventative and interventional.

Consequences of Tormenting Tangible Grace

The human body as tangible grace is vulnerable to physical, mental, emotional, and spiritual harm. The experience of the body of a teenager who's in a violent romantic relationship is one of torment. What are the physical, mental, and spiritual consequences of the teenage body being tormented?

Jacquelyn C. Campbell, PhD, a registered nurse and scholar, writes about the consequences of intimate-partner violence against women of all ages. Her research about adults informs us about consequences of intimate-partner violence for teenagers. Sexual and/or physical assault results in the most common mental and physical health-care issues. From 1985 to 1998, intimate-partner violence cases made up 4 to 23 percent of investigations in US health-care settings, with the lowest prevalence among middle-level socioeconomic and well-educated groups, and the higher prevalence among poorer women and girls.[20] Intimate-partner violence usually results in "long-term negative health consequences for survivors, even after the abuse has ended."[21] Campbell writes, "Battered women and girls are more likely to have been injured in the head, face, neck, thorax, breasts, and abdomen than women injured in other ways." Forced sex or rape results in gynecological problems that include sexually transmitted diseases, vaginal bleeding, fibroids, and urinary-tract infections.[22] "The main health effect specific to abuse during pregnancy is the threat to health and risk of death of the mother, fetus, or both from trauma."[23] Campbell lists depression, post-traumatic stress disorder, and alcohol and drug abuse as the three main mental health effects of intimate-partner violence.[24] Statistics show that 40 to 60 percent of murders of women and girls in North America are perpetrated by intimate partners.[25]

Marsha Wood and Christine Barter, researchers and policy experts, examined intimate-partner violence among teenage mothers during pregnancy. They interviewed sixteen teenage mothers in the United Kingdom as part of a wider study on intimate-partner violence in the relationships of disadvantaged young people. Their research found an increased risk of intimate-partner violence during pregnancy and motherhood. As with adult mothers, so with teenage mothers who experience violence during pregnancy: consequences for them and their fetus/child include "low birth weight, increased fetal and maternal mortality, and greater risks of miscarriage."[26] It is important to note how Wood and Barter's research describes the disadvantaged backgrounds of pregnant teens and teen mothers. They indicate these girls experience financial insecurity and isolation from supportive networks. These teenage girls chose to get pregnant with hopes of lifting themselves from poverty and not to obtain state benefits, as they are usually stereotyped as doing.[27] Wood and Barter's examination of the experiences of teen mothers and the main consequences of intimate-partner violence echoes Campbell's research: These teen girls experience physical, sexual, and emotional abuse.

Caitlin Wolford-Clevenger, a psychology professor at the University of Tennessee, Knoxville, and her colleagues sought to understand the relationship between dating violence and suicidal thoughts among college students as a way of providing appropriate intervention. They note, "Dating violence victimization, particularly physical assault and psychological aggression, is a well-documented risk factor for suicidal thoughts in men and women."[28] These authors found that dating violence victimization is particularly pervasive among college students. Statistics relevant to college students who are older adolescents are relevant to teenagers. College student relationships made up 37 percent of physical assaults and 90 percent of instances of psychological aggression. Wolford-Clevenger's research with older adolescents is relevant for teenagers who are considered in the middle of the adolescent age group.

The torment of a teen's spirit also is a consequence of teen dating violence. This means we must also consider the spiritual life of a teen who experiences dating violence. How does a girl feel about herself after repeated physical and sexual abuse by her partner? How does she feel about God? She may feel she deserves the violence, that it is God's will for her life. Or she may feel the violence is God's punishment for not obeying or pleasing her partner.

Viewing violence as normal suggests a belief that God ordains one's abuse and suffering. When such religious beliefs collude with economic stressors, rationalizing violence in an intimate relationship as ordained by God is prevalent. A poor young mother's dependence on her partner exacerbates the likelihood of her being abused at the hands of her partner.[29] Becky, one of the teen mothers in Wood and Baxter's research project, talked about ending her relationship with her very controlling partner but felt she may return to him due to "financial difficulties, isolation, and poor housing that she was experiencing as a single mother."[30] Young, disadvantaged mothers may view violence as a more integral or normal aspect of their relationships.[31] These teen mothers suggest that they have no viable choices for survival but to stay with an abusive partner if they want food and shelter. The thoughts behind such actions are pessimistic and hopeless, indicators of a downtrodden and broken spirit. Beliefs that dating violence is normal indicate an understanding that God or a divine being created partners to be in violent relationships.

On the other hand, when a young mother is left with no other financially secure options but to stay in an abusive relationship, her spirit is beaten into submission by patriarchal beliefs. Enduring controlling behavior of an abusive partner and viewing such behavior as normal or ordained by God is evidence of a spirit tormented by patriarchy—the domineering and controlling power and privilege that gives men authority to subordinate women and girls culturally, economically, and sexually.[32] "Power and privilege given to men in a patriarchal society," writes New Testament and ethics scholar Miranda Pillay, are "justified and sanctified by culture and religion."[33] The pervasiveness of this understanding, says Pillay, means that women and girls often "either choose to or have no choice in performing their expected gender roles steeped in subservience; and men assume headship roles in the grand narrative of patriarchal heteronormativity as the *natural order of things*."[34] The silencing and powerlessness that patriarchy promotes, she says, wounds the spirit of women and girls. The patriarchal nature of the Christian church continues to torment the spirits of teenagers who experience intimate violence and believe that abuse they receive is of God.[35]

Tangible Grace, Gender, and Communion as Love

In an effort to help teenagers, and young adult women in particular, navigate a patriarchal world to find love, educator and feminist cultural critic bell hooks wrote *Communion: The Female Search for Love*. The book gleans women's wisdom and experiences of what it means to love. The book defies patriarchal culture while urging young women to move beyond old patriarchal versions of love to new meanings of love "as a transformational force demanding of each individual accountability and responsibility for nurturing our spiritual growth."[36] The importance of her book is in its discussion of true freedom for young women to find love. hooks writes, "We bear witness to that truth that no female can find freedom without first finding her way to love."[37] Self-love is the starting point for finding love. Committing to the work of learning to value yourself, to recognize your self-worth, and to create positive self-esteem is the starting point for loving toward freedom.[38] Her words provide a pathway for young women to work for and receive love that is not tethered by patriarchal ways of knowing and enacting love relationships.

True communion—the ability and activity of loving one's self and another—brings freedom to be fully a person who loves their body, their mind, and their spirit. When one loves one's self, one is free to love another regardless of whether the lovers are two cisgender or nonbinary females or two cisgender or nonbinary males. Communion as love transcends socialized notions of gender. Communion as love gives the human spirit energy and power to connect with the Spirit of the divine. God is Spirit, in the Christian tradition, and we worship God in spirit and truth (John 4:24). The Holy Spirit, God dwelling in the world today and within our bodies, is love. John continues to write about the indwelling of the Spirit and love from Jesus's perspective: "I in them and you in me, that they may become . . . one, so that the world may know that you have sent me and have loved them even as you have loved me" (John 17:23). Here John argues for an understanding of the Spirit as love in conjunction with the Triune God who acts as one, which means, as Adonis Vidu writes, "that the indivisibility of divine triune action . . . do[es] not undertake separate actions. . . . One cannot even individuate distinct actions of the persons."[39] While this argument is debatable, the point that the Triune God dwells in our bodies as love is worth noting. John writes in 14:22–23 that Judas (not Iscariot) said to Jesus, "Lord, how is it that you will reveal yourself to us, and not to the world?" Jesus answers him, "Those who love me will keep my word, and my Father will love them, and we will come to them and make our home with them."

God the Father, Jesus the Savior, and the Spirit as Advocate come as three persons in one to be Divine Love dwelling within us. The indwelling Spirit of God is connected to the love the Triune God brings into our bodies, the temples of God.[40]

This turn toward the indwelling Triune God who brings love—communion—to our bodies empowers young women and girls to love themselves as God loves. Such communion opposes the self-hatred that patriarchal culture promotes.[41] Communion as love becomes release from being a superwoman, tough as nails, or one who declares one is in love with work or one's sport instead of another human being. Communion as love brings wholeness to a teenager's love, in so doing creating a bridge for wholesome communion with another person, a wholesome communion with a lover.

Communion as love enables one to express love intimately through touching the self and one's beloved. The intimate touching of the tangible grace that young lovers share, the caressing and cuddling of skin on skin, transports young lovers not only to a physical but also to a spiritual realm. Indeed, love expressed in coitus or lovemaking is transcendent. By this I mean that lovers who understand and believe in the scaredness of sexual intercourse and engage in the activity of lovemaking are transcendent in body and spirit during those very moments. Lovemaking has the power to transport them to a divine spiritual realm. The ecstasy of physical lovemaking is tantamount to spiritual ecstasy. The erotic words from the Song of Solomon illustrate the intimacy of touchable tangible grace. "My beloved is to me a bag of myrrh that lies between my breasts. My beloved is to me a cluster of henna blossoms in the vineyards of En-gedi" (1:13–14).

Religious leaders—youth pastors/ministers—must affirm and celebrate love that manifests as intimate touching among teenagers. They must stress the importance of being mature and responsible for the emotional and psychological aspects of engaging in physical intimacy. When youth leaders do not raise teens' awareness about the sacredness of intimate touching and their responsibility for maintaining that sacredness, teens are at risk of psychologically and emotionally tormenting their romantic partner. At that point, communion as love is distorted.

Tangible Grace, Dating, and Race

Race and ethnicity in dating and intimate touching, particularly among teenagers, are not factors to be ignored. In today's society, interracial dating is increasingly common, yet the problem of race and racism still persists. As such, it is important to briefly consider dating, touching, and race as we think about teens, intimate relationships, and partner violence.

Intimate touching among European and African-descended women and men has been a contested conversation in the United States since Europeans' colonization of the land. Intimate touching between Native American women and white settlers was relatively rare but usually violent as white settlers raped Native American women and girls, and pillaged and burned their villages. On the other hand, history indicates there were a few Native American men who chose to woo white women. John "Kooweskoowe" Ross, the chief of the Cherokee people from the 1820s until 1866, assisted in developing laws against intermarriage between Cherokee women and white men.[42] After the death of his Cherokee wife, Kooweskoowe himself courted white women in elite circles. He met and fell in love with Mary Brown Stapler from Wilmington, Delaware. He referred to their courtship as his "treaty," chronicled in letters he sent Mary. Their eventual marriage became considered as one of "America's epic romance stories."[43]

Laws that regulated intimate touching are documented in the *Loving v. Virginia* case against interracial marriage laws. During their teen years in high school, Mildred Loving, a young woman of African descent, and Richard Loving, a white man, met and fell in love while growing up in rural Central Point in Caroline County, Virginia. Their clandestine courtship led to a deeper commitment of engagement and lovemaking that led to Mildred becoming pregnant in 1958. The couple decided to get married and went to Washington, DC, to legalize their commitment within the law.

Upon returning to Virginia, their marriage became public knowledge, and authorities invaded the privacy of their home in the early morning hours in hopes of catching them having sex, which was another illegal practice in Virginia between people of different races. Mildred pointed the policemen to their marriage license hanging on their bedroom wall, but the license was not acknowledged. The police arrested Richard and Mildred. Richard was sentenced to one year in prison for violating Virginia's Racial Integrity Act of 1924, which forbade whites and colored persons from marrying one another. In response, Mildred wrote letters to civil rights lawyers for help in recognizing their legal marriage. In 1967, the Supreme Court ruled in the Lovings' favor, and the court's decision led to the dismantling of antimiscegenation laws in the United States. The Black-and-white love of Mildred and Richard produced six children.[44] Black on white skin, intimately and lovingly touching, eventually transformed the landscape of US legal practices of Black and white skin touching. Intimate touching as love, which can begin during teen years, has long-standing implications for race, gender, and sexuality.

Overview of the Book

I explore the above issues of teenage dating violence as a womanist practical theologian, which means I am a Black feminist concerned about issues of race, gender, class, and sexual identity as I consider lived religious beliefs of girls and young adult women. I posit that embodied religious beliefs are shaped by context, which includes socioeconomic, sociopolitical, and sociocultural forces. My theological reflections and the questions that generate them are shaped by my womanist perspective.

The chapters that follow use the idea of tangible grace and torment to problematize contexts of teen dating violence. Each chapter begins with a story or vignette of an experienced religious leader whom I interviewed, either in the Western Cape of South Africa or in Texas and Florida in the United States. The focus of each chapter—whether teaching, preaching/sacred rhetoric, liturgy/worship, pastoral care, or advocacy—is captured in the vignette of the chapter. Each chapter homes in on a problem framed through the idea of tormenting teens' tangible grace as a kind of second movement. As the third movement of each chapter, I turn to best practices for preventing and intervening in teen dating violence. These best practices include models of teaching, preaching, worshipping, pastoral care, and advocacy with youth already in violent romantic relationships or those at risk of teen dating violence.

Chapter 1 examines best practices for intervening and preventing teen dating violence through teaching. First, I begin with a vignette of a phenomenal teacher from the Muslim religious tradition who teaches teens and their mothers about gender-based violence in the context of human sexuality classes. Second, I focus on teaching against the tormenting of tangible grace of youth by examining the problems of current curricula in congregations. Elliott Eisner's idea of three curricula (explicit, implicit, and null) guides my argument. I show that many congregations and nonprofit religious institutions practice implicit and/or null curricula, and explore the harm this does. Then follows a section on best practices about the role of religions leaders in preventing and intervening in teen dating violence.[45] Common to most of those interventions is teaching about human sexuality as a method of preventing and intervening in teen dating violence.

Chapter 2 focuses on the formative nature of preaching to youth about teen dating violence in contexts where their faith is formed. The chapter begins with an actual event that happened while a sermon on gender-based violence was being given. I show how important preaching and religious rhetoric are in the faith formation of youth. I interrogate preaching that deforms the faith of youth, noting that this is a way of tormenting the tangible body of a youth. Ethical preaching to congregations that considers gender-based violence is preaching that is accountable by promoting healthy and wholesome faith formation. I offer practical ways to preach ethically and responsibly, and coupled with this suggest how the congregation—including youth—reflecting together on the sermon with the preacher can hold everyone accountable.

Chapter 3, on liturgy and worship, begins with an original poem written for liturgy during worship by a pastor. It considers liturgy and worship, focusing specifically on the role of worship in faith formation of youth at risk for or in violent romantic relationships, and the irony and contradiction of tormented tangible grace in worship. I wonder about how a person and specifically a teenager suffering from violent abuse by an intimate partner might experience the so-called celebration of the Christian sacrament of Eucharist, and how we might need to change our practices. The chapter concludes with a worship service of hope on ending teen gender-based violence.

Chapter 4 addresses pastoral care and counseling. While all the religious leaders I interviewed in both South Africa and the United States had not had a youth come to them expressing concerns about violence in their dating relationships, some of those leaders had experienced teens confessing their experiences of teen dating violence publicly in workshops, retreats, and confirmation classes. The chapter begins with the experience of a pastor who raised a teen couple's awareness of intimate partner violence while counseling them ahead of their wedding. This story is relevant to pastoral concerns for addressing trauma caused by intimate-partner violence because it demonstrates how such settings can reveal the possibility of teen gender-based violence. Trauma and the tormenting of tangible grace are natural twins that require an exploration of injury and harm caused by intimate-partner violence as well as serve as a launching point for best practices in pastoral care for teens at risk of or involved in teen dating violence.

Chapter 5 focuses on advocacy and policy making on behalf of teens at risk of relationship violence or already in violent romantic relationships. Here advocacy refers to any kind of intervention or service to end violence in youth romantic relationships. This chapter uses service as the starting point for the discussion and the theological umbrella for exploring policy making as a solution to tormented tangible grace. The chapter begins with my own story of engagement with young computer experts who worked to prevent gender-based violence in South Africa. I consider the tormenting of tangible grace through the lenses of policy making and policy implementation with youth. The objective of this chapter is to give religious leaders skills and resources to advocate with and on behalf of youth against gender-based violence.

My hope is for this book to inspire readers to advocate for youth in ways that help prevent and intervene in teen dating violence. Partnerships with practitioners who are committed to preventing and intervening in youth partner violence are important. This is a divine vocation that our divine, tangible bodies are called to engage. The future thriving of teens in our youth groups, teens in our high school classrooms, and young adults on our college campuses depend on our speaking the truth about teen dating violence and the related problems of patriarchy and power that harm God's gift of tangible grace.

Notes

1. Al Miles, *Ending Violence in Teen Dating Relationships: A Resource Guide for Parents and Pastors* (Fortress, 2005). Miles discusses denial of teen dating violence on 102–7.
2. I use *teenagers* and *youth* interchangeably because in 2019 I interviewed interfaith religious leaders in South Africa, more specifically in the region of Cape Town, where fifteen- to twenty-four-year-olds are considered youth. In 2020 I interviewed interfaith religious leaders in Texas and Florida, who speak of this age cohort as teenagers and young adults. Psychosocial development literature identifies them as middle and older adolescents.
3. The CDC does not specify an age for teens. It refers to high school age in its materials on teen dating violence. One of its publications, "Dating Matters: Strategies to Promote Healthy Teen Relationships," targets eleven to fourteen years of age, indicating middle school and high school.
4. Evelyn L. Parker, "Honor the Body," in *On Our Way: Christian Practices for Living a Whole Life*, ed. Dorothy C. Bass and Susan Briehl (Upper Room Books, 2010).
5. Parker, "Honor the Body."
6. Serene Jones, *Call It Grace: Finding Meaning in a Fractured World* (Viking Books, 2019).
7. Jones, *Call It Grace*, xviii.

8. From blind or visually impaired people nonetheless come amazing sculptures and paintings, and from hearing-impaired persons we hear amazing music and see amazing theatrical performances. Take Michael Williams, an African American from Nashville. He has received numerous awards for his paintings, including an award from President Obama, despite his Stargart's disease, which is a macular degenerative disease. Halle Berry, the first African American woman to receive an Oscar for Best Actress, lost 80 percent of her hearing in her left ear after a blow to her head during a domestic violence incident in a previous relationship. Or take Matthew Whitaker, a blind sixteen-year-old piano prodigy who has performed on keyboard worldwide, playing music ranging from classical, to pop, to rhythm and blues, to gospel. He is among many others who are sight- and/or hearing-impaired child prodigies. Human bodies that we deem to be abnormal were created within the mysterious realm of perfection through God's Divine Love, *grace*.

9. Jones, *Call It Grace*, xviii.

10. Stephanie Paulsell, "Honoring the Body," in *Practicing Our Faith: A Way of Life for a Searching People*, ed. Dorothy C. Bass (Wiley & Sons, 2009), 18.

11. Paulsell, "Honoring the Body," 22–23.

12. Michael Cole and Sheila R. Cole, *The Development of Children* (Scientific American Books, 1989), 174.

13. Susan M. Sanders, *Teen Dating Violence: The Invisible Peril* (Peter Lang, 2003), 95.

14. Sanders, *Teen Dating Violence*, 97.

15. Sanders, *Teen Dating Violence*, 98.

16. Sanders, *Teen Dating Violence*, 98–100.

17. Sanders, *Teen Dating Violence*, 79.

18. Sanders, *Teen Dating Violence*, 84.

19. Sanders, *Teen Dating Violence*, 84.

20. Jacquelyn Campbell, *Assessing Dangerousness: Violence by Batterers and Child Abusers*, 2nd ed. (Springer, 2007), 1331.

21. Campbell, *Assessing Dangerousness*, 1331.

22. Campbell, *Assessing Dangerousness*, 1332.

23. Campbell, *Assessing Dangerousness*, 1333.

24. Campbell, *Assessing Dangerousness*, 1334.

25. Campbell, *Assessing Dangerousness*, 1331.

26. Marsha Wood and Christine Barter, "Hopes and Fears: Teenage Mothers' Experiences of Intimate Partner Violence," *Children & Society* 29, no. 6 (2015): 558–68, https://doi.org/10.1111/chso.12100.

27. Wood and Barter, "Hopes and Fears."

28. Caitlin Wolford-Clevenger, JoAnna Elmquist, Meagan Brem, Heather Zapor, and Gregory L. Stuart, "Dating Violence Victimization, Interpersonal Needs, and Suicidal Ideation Among College Students," *Crisis: The Journal of Crisis Intervention and Suicide Prevention* 37, no. 1 (2016): 51, https://doi.org/10.1027/0227-5910/a000353.

29. Wood and Baxter, "Hopes and Fears," 560.

30. Wood and Baxter, "Hopes and Fears," 560.

31. Wood and Baxter, "Hopes and Fears," 561.

32. Miranda Pillay, "The Church, Gender and AIDS: What's Wrong with Patriarchy?," *Missionalia* 43, no. 3 (2015): 558–67.

33. Pillay, "The Church, Gender, and AIDS," 560.

34. Pillay, "The Church, Gender, and AIDS," 560.

35. Pillay, "The Church, Gender, and AIDS," 560. Unfortunately, for centuries the church has promoted and continues to promote patriarchy in its educational and liturgical practices. When religious leaders preach and teach biblical texts on relationships between women and men, or on expected roles of each, without critiquing patriarchal ideologies culturally woven into the Scriptures, they are aiding and abetting persons and behaviors that harm the bodies and spirits of women and girls. More egregious is resistance or reluctance to teach or preach texts that give voice to voiceless raped and abused victims in our congregations. The rape of Tamar in 2 Sam 13, the rape and dismemberment of the body of the unnamed woman in Judges 19–20, and the gang rape of an unnamed woman in Gen 19 are all texts of horrific rape cases, or what Phyllis Trible calls "texts of terror" in the HB/OT. Rape comes out of a patriarchal ideology of violent sexual perversion and abuse of power. Religious leaders who intentionally resist teaching and preaching these texts perpetuate the silence of women and girls in their congregations whose voices have been dimmed or silenced by abusive men who claim their power and authority from the patriarchal religious institution, which is the church.

The patriarchal church promotes the wounding of the spirits of women and girls and thereby harms the Spirit of God. I have written that our bodies—tangible embodiments of grace—have the capacity to hold and reveal the Holy Spirit. Paul asks the bickering congregation at Corinth twice, "Do you not know that you are God's temple and that God's Spirit dwells in you?" He goes on to urge the Corinthian congregation to "glorify God in your body," hoping the congregation will honor God by honoring their bodies and the bodies of others as the dwelling place of the Spirit (1 Cor 3:16, 6:19–20).

The human body was created to shelter the Holy Spirit, who yearns to dwell in communion with our spirit—the two together in our bodies.

36. bell hooks, *Communion: The Female Search for Love* (HarperCollins, 2002), xviii.

37. hooks, *Communion*, xviii.

38. hooks, *Communion*, 221.

39. Adonis Vidu, "The Indwelling of the Holy Spirit as Love," in *The Same God Who Works All Things* (Eerdmans, 2021), 12.

40. Vidu, "Indwelling of the Holy Spirit," 12.

41. hooks, *Communion*, xviii.

42. Ann McGrath, "Making Love—and Nations," Sapiens, February 14, 2016, https://www.sapiens.org/culture/making-love-and-nations/.

43. McGrath, "Making Love—and Nations."

44. The *Loving v. Virginia* story is recorded in many forms, including books and movies. There are other, less well-known stories of miscegenation in the history of US that merit research.

45. Interviews from South Africa were supported by my 2019 Fulbright Scholarship. Interviews in the US were supported by the Southern Methodist University Scholarly Outreach Award I, 2020–2021.

CHAPTER ONE

Teaching and the Implicit Curriculum

She came into my house draped in red, blue plaid, and cream. Her cream-colored hijab softly framed a face expressing wisdom and strength. Her voice was strong, yet she spoke in quiet tones that indicated enthusiasm about teaching. Her students were Muslim mothers and their children, both boys and girls. She taught them courses on human sexuality that gave attention to issues of gender-based violence in relationships. She was invested in girls and boys understanding the relationship between human sexuality and sacred texts in the Qur'an. More specifically, she was determined to affirm their humanity and the humanity of all people created by Allah.

Magboeba David is a laywoman, a Muslim, a mother, a wife, and a teacher. She teaches Muslim mothers and their children in mosques as well as people of all religious perspectives in interfaith workshops and through a weekly radio program. Her passion and commitment to teaching against gender-based violence is an apt starting point to discuss teaching as a practice to prevent and intervene in teen dating violence.

Teaching is the intentional facilitation of learning through engagement with students and teachers offering content in a particular context. The aim of teaching is not simply for students to consume content for personal gratification. For it to have integrity, teaching must lead to transformation of systematic injustices, including gender-based violence.

I offer this definition of teaching unapologetically as a teacher who professes teaching to have emancipatory or liberating potential. I teach and write about teaching in the tradition of Paulo Freire, a Brazilian educator and author of the seminal book *Pedagogy of the Oppressed.*[1] A long list of notable scholars espouse education as liberatory, including bell hooks in *Teaching to Transgress.*[2] Some contemporary scholars, such as Johnathan Jodamus, Megan Robertson, and Sarojini Nadar, show the complexity of education as liberation and deepen earlier notions of teaching to argue for a "socially just pedagogy."[3] Their pedagogical position merits quoting: "A socially just pedagogy, which is facilitated through critical, queer, liberatory, and feminist pedagogies intentionally focuses on the 'what' and the 'how' of knowledge where a consideration of power is key to shaping how we teach."[4] Teaching against gender-based violence necessitates the type of teaching that addresses power imbalances in society. To teach against teen dating violence requires a socially just pedagogy understood as an emancipatory education.

Teaching against the tormenting of tangible grace requires addressing implicit curriculum in the home and in religious institutions. Many institutions have appropriated Eisner's notion of three curricula structuring an educational setting, as mentioned in the introduction above: the explicit, implicit, and null curricula.[5] The explicit curriculum refers to what is actually presented and taught to students/learners. The implicit or implied curriculum is the hidden or less obvious and unintentional content that is taught unreflectively through habits and assumptions. Examples of implicit curriculum are white and patriarchal assumptions. Null curriculum is content that teaches because it is absent, intentionally left out, erased, and denied. An example of null curriculum is historical facts about the plight of African-descended people in the United States that have been erased from history books. For example, the Texas State Board of Education debated omitting the use of the term *slavery*, to be replaced by *involuntary relocation*, in second-grade social studies curriculum. While the Board of Education rejected the implementation of the change, if it had it been accepted or not discussed at all it would have been an example of the null curriculum.[6]

While we can use Eisner's theory to discuss all three types of curricula in relationship to the tormenting of youth's tangible grace in violent romantic relationships, I want to focus on how hidden curriculum in family and religious institutions perpetuates gender-based violence. The father who constantly berates his children's mother in front of them by calling her stupid and ignorant teaches them that mothers are not intellectually equal to fathers. The children may unwittingly absorb and adopt these understandings of their mother—until perhaps they mature sufficiently to evaluate critically the characteristics their father has ascribed to their mother (and up until now they have as well). Children, regardless of their own gender, implicitly learn that women are intellectually inferior to the men. A similar situation can occur in families with same-gender parents. If one parent refers to the other with derogatory language, such as calling their partner stupid or ignorant, the child(ren) may adopt the same language in reference to that parent and thus also become complicit in abusing the parent psychologically through implicit learning.

Another example of the implicit curriculum of gender-based violence in the home is physical abuse of the mother/parent, such as slapping, punching, pinching, poking, and any other forms of physical abuse. Such acts teach the children that physically abusing a mother/parent is somehow normal. If the mother/parent fights back, the implicit lesson is that physical fighting among parents is normal and thus acceptable. What children learn from the implicit curriculum of how parents engage each other in the home is an aspect of their learning how parents behave in relationship.

Consider the implicit curriculum in the context of a Christian church. Building on Eisner, Christian religious educator Maria Harris argues that curriculum is the "entire course of the church's life."[7] She discusses five areas of the church's curriculum: preaching, community, prayer/liturgy/worship, teaching/learning, and troublemaking/social justice/service. If we consider the curriculum of a church in this way, we can think of examples of the implicit curriculum of gender-based violence, affecting minds, bodies, and spirits.

Statistics show that one in every twelve high schoolers experiences physical and sexual dating violence.[8] Extrapolate that to a large group such as a congregation with a large percentage of teenagers, and one quickly gets an idea of the extent of the problem. Some might be sitting in the worship service with heavy makeup and dark glasses to cover the bruises on their faces. Some girls sitting in worship might have been sexually or physically abused by their boyfriends just a few hours earlier while on a date. Yet in many churches the Sunday school lesson, sermon, and liturgy imply women and girls' absolute obedience to male authority in all relationships, including intimate ones. Although not written, the indirect message that is sent through practices conveys that women and girls should accept violence from men and boys in obedience to male authority. This is an example of the implicit curriculum that teaches children and youth to obey male authority without thinking critically about obedience to male authority or about who has vested that authority in males.

When the Sunday school lesson, sermon, liturgy, and music in a worship service do not speak to a teenage girl's experiences of intimate-partner violence, we call that a null curriculum. The very absence of the topic teaches all congregants, particularly children and youth, because words about violence against women and girls are missing. The very absence of affirmation of the humanity of women and girls in music and liturgy implies that they are somehow inhumane. Youth learn or can assume through the church's very avoidance of the topic that violence against females is permissible. Likewise, when inclusion or mention of same-gender-loving nonbinary or cisgender persons is avoided in a worship service, the very absence of the words teaches that such persons are inhumane or invisible.

Such implicit and null curricula present a challenge to emancipatory pedagogy about tormented tangible grace, in that there is no liberative teaching about gender-based violence that could free and motivate congregants, particularly children and youth, to stand against gender-based violence. Children and youth do not necessarily have the critical knowledge, skills, maturity, or self-differentiation yet to recognize and act appropriately when threatened by egregious acts of violence that will injure their bodies, minds, and spirits. With those realities in mind, we can examine various forms of emancipatory pedagogy that can disrupt the implicit and null curricula of gender-based violence.

Human Sexuality as an Education Umbrella

For over twenty years, Magboeba David has been using her human sexuality classes on the radio and in mosques as opportunities to include content about gender-based violence. Thanks to this longevity, she has built trust among the families of the Muslim community who listen to her broadcasts and attend her sessions. Specifically, she has taught courses titled Pathway to Manhood and Pathway to Womanhood for slightly more than ten years. In them, she carefully weaves physiological and biological information about male and female anatomy into her sessions, including passages from the Qur'an to remind hearers of the sacredness of the human body. Her PowerPoint presentation titled Pathway to Womanhood includes a slide that shows how abused women and girls feel powerless because they are being controlled. Another slide broaches the topic of how staying in an abusive relationship perpetuates fear within a woman or girl, a fear Magboeba terms the "golden handcuff syndrome." In addition to human sexuality courses, she has lectured in interfaith forums and spoken on panels about the problem of gender-based violence in the Western Cape region of South Africa.

Magboeba's practice is like that of other clergy and religious leaders who believe that teaching young people about aspects of gender-based violence happens best in human sexuality classes.[9] Many religious leaders suggest that the topic is too difficult to stand alone in religious teaching and learning contexts and should be embedded in human sexuality courses until students and parents realize the importance of allowing standalone courses. Rev. Dr. Andy Stoker, senior pastor of Central United Methodist Church, Albuquerque, believes that a robust human sexuality program and dating curriculum are good practices and vehicles by which to address teen dating violence. He posits that thinking theologically about every aspect of our beings, even as sexual beings, is important. Teaching critical thinking about the theological underpinnings of human sexuality is the best approach, according to Rev. Stoker. His theological touchpoint of *imago Dei*—being created in God's image—is essential to his teaching materials on human sexuality and dating. He has also used United Methodist Church–approved curriculum on human sexuality and finds it flexible enough for him to possibly incorporate an additional module on gender-based violence for teens.

However, the challenge regarding teaching about gender-based violence in human sexuality courses is that many religious communities or institutions do not espouse or practice teaching human sexuality, thus not providing an avenue for teaching about gender-based violence with teenagers. The reality is that teaching human sexuality to youth is not thought to be as important as it was in 1990, when I was director of youth and children's ministries at Northaven United Methodist

Church in Dallas. The broader topic of human sexuality was then being addressed in conversations about homosexuality in progressive Christian congregations. Since then, the United Methodist Church has fractured over passionate debates about ordaining queer clergy and presiding over queer marriages. The vitriolic debates about human sexuality halt most, if not all, conversations about teaching human sexuality to youth in most Protestant churches. Yet teaching human sexuality to youth is as critical today as it has ever been. Thus, the question about teaching youth about gender-based violence in human sexuality classes prompts the question of when, where, and how to teach about human sexuality.[10]

What is human sexuality education? It entails "learning about all aspects of sexuality and how it changes throughout our lifetime."[11] Religious beliefs, teachings about our bodies, and our relationships all shape how we understand our sexuality over time.[12] Those who teach about sexuality usually cover five broad areas: sexual health and reproduction, sensuality, intimacy, sexual identity, and sexualization.[13] Each offers ways to connect with aspects of gender-based violence. Sexual health and reproduction addresses concerns about the biological and physiological aspects of the body. Sensuality concerns how our bodies respond to pleasure physically. Intimacy is emotional closeness to another person and to God, and how that closeness is reciprocated. Sexual identity is how we understand or identify ourselves as female, male, queer, or nonbinary. And sexualization is the way in which sexuality is used for good or ill, specifically regarding power and control. In one form or another, all these areas are connected to our faith, our bodies, and our relationships, and therefore they also have to do with gender-based violence among teenagers. Engaging in human sexuality education assists in understanding gender-based violence and how that understanding might best be taught in a religious context.

The context for teaching gender-based violence as a module in human sexuality curriculum is important, for context affects the nature of curriculum content. When considering how to teach gender-based violence in a human sexuality course, ask yourself: What are the ages, developmental stages, and experiences of the students? How do the students identify themselves regarding gender, sexuality, class? Will the adult caregivers of the students be present? If so, how will the lessons or sessions be designed to include the various levels of maturity and power? What is the optimal time for effectively teaching a module on gender-based violence—both in terms of the length of the session and the time in a youth's life?

Educating About the Impact of Patriarchy

While including discussion of gender-based violence in human sexuality programs is important, raising awareness about the human body, patriarchy, power, sexism, and other topics relevant to gender-based violence is crucial too, since these touch on the underlying power dynamics. The Torah, the Qur'an, and the Bible provide excellent content for addressing the problem of gender-based violence by first addressing the causative phenomena—principally patriarchy and power/authority—for gender-based violence. Teaching the holy Scripture subversively toward awareness is one way to teach indirectly about systems/structures that enable gender-based violence. How leaders in the Old Testament used their power is a good starting point for subversive teaching about power that typically undergirds violence against women and girls. For example, trace the use of power during the reign of David in 2 Samuel. Notice the use of power in his relationships with his wives, concubines, daughters, and other women. Select texts for discussion to problematize King David's use of power. Ask: Who benefits from his power? How? Who is harmed? How? How is David's power indicative of patriarchy more broadly?

Consider teaching Old Testament texts that reify violence against women and girls. Jewish women, specifically Jewish feminist scholars, have paved the way for teaching about violence against women and girls from Hebrew Scripture.[14] Their scholarship includes exploration of sexual and other violence against women in Hebrew narratives as well as violence against women in biblical law.[15] The violence against Jephthah's daughter in Judges 11:1–12:7 is an example of the senseless killing of a young girl due to a senseless promise of her father. The narrative is a good example of femicide—killing a girl or woman because her gender is less valuable than and unequal to male gender. Even though Jephthah's reckless decision may have been related to the trauma that he received as a rejected child born of a prostitute, the story is tangled with violence related to gender-related assessment of who is worthy or unworthy, and of whether and how family members recognize that. This text has all the ingredients useful for emancipatory pedagogy about gender-based violence with teens and adults.

Teaching Strategies as Prevention and Intervention

Teaching to help prevent and intervene in teen dating violence can be done in many ways. Gleaning from best practices from various religious leaders who teach about teen gender-based violence, I recommend three areas of teaching: a module on gender-based violence education that is part of a broader human sexuality education; teaching about power, authority, and patriarchy through subversive readings of holy Scriptures; and teaching about teen dating violence in neutral spaces.

A Module Within Human Sexuality Education
Once we understand the concept of human sexuality education and the place of gender-based violence education in it, then we can address the content of the gender-based violence module. Here are guidelines for content development:

1. Determine an overarching focus or aim of the module, then the number of sessions to be taught, and the focus and learning objectives for each session. For example, focusing on identifying healthy and unhealthy relationships over two three-hour sessions on two consecutive days can be ideal for teaching a module in an appropriate public school course at the invitation of a teacher.[16]
2. Design experiential activities that correlate to the learning objectives. Experiential learning activities involve learning by doing or learning through reflection on doing an activity.[17] Think of multisensory activities that involve the use of sight, sound, smell, touch, and taste experiences with abstract concepts and ideas.
3. Integrate into your activities and teaching relevant key concepts and definitions, such as patriarchy, power, relationships, and empathy.
4. Integrate theological concepts in the activities. Relevant religious practices about honoring the body are essential to a gender-based violence module. Determine what honoring the body means for Muslim, Jewish, traditional African spirituality, or other religious traditions. For example, the Christian practice of honoring the body is essential to the central concept of tangible grace.
5. Design evaluation activities that assess your learning objectives. Ideally, evaluation activities are included throughout the teaching session but should certainly occur at the end of the session. Another method of assessment is the use of a pre- and post-test.

Scripture and Subversive Teaching

See the above discussion about teaching subversively using Scripture under 'Educating About the Impact of Patriarchy." Focus on power and patriarchy in biblical passages to emphasize the importance of critical thinking about these areas.

Teaching in Neutral Spaces

There are neutral spaces beyond religious congregations and religious institutions that affirm and invite curriculum on gender-based violence with youth. Here is an outline of a session plan, which can be the first in a series of two or three sessions, for teachers in such contexts.

Preparation: Follow steps 1–3 above.

Aim or Focus of Module: The module raises students' awareness of gender-based violence.

This Session's Focus: This session focuses on healthy relationships. It is usually the first in a series of two or three sessions.

Session Objectives:

1. To conceptualize or define the term *relationship*
2. To differentiate types of relationships
3. To construct a model or plan for assessing and forming healthy relationships, particularly healthy romantic relationships

Activity 1: Invite students to brainstorm words or phrases that represent their understanding of the word *relationship*. Students can respond verbally or write their word or phrase on a board or flip chart. Engage the students in conversations about their responses. Affirm all responses to encourage participation of all students. Organize the responses under various categories that include family and friends, healthy and unhealthy, and so on. Most words will appear in several categories. Invite students to tell short stories to illustrate a response under each category.

Activity 2: Invite students to create human machines to represent examples of good or healthy relationships. Their human machines can have moving parts and make sounds.[18] Debrief the experience asking questions about feelings. Ask whether their definition of good relationships has changed as a result of the activity, and if so, how.

Activity 3: Invite students to form groups of three and draw a three-frame cartoon about how a character finds and forms a healthy relationship. Invite students to display and present their cartoons. Be prepared to take a walking tour of each cartoon to hear the authors' presentations.

Wrap-Up and Reflection: Schedule time to reflect on the activities of the session. Focus on how students understand healthy relationships. Also, have students discuss how they plan to identify persons with whom they can have healthy relationships and how to avoid unhealthy relationships, especially unhealthy romantic ones. However, discuss romantic relationships only if appropriate. Do not force this level of understanding regarding relationships except to set up the next session.

Writing Prayers

In honor of February as Teen Dating Violence Awareness Month, read and reflect on 2 Samuel 13:1–22. Realizing that women and girls experience sexual violence every day, and five women with disabilities are raped daily,[19] write a prayer for the victims and perpetrators of sexual violence that might be in your own congregation or context. Use the ACTS model (adoration, confession, thanksgiving, supplication) to organize each paragraph of your prayer.

After writing your prayer, share it with another youth pastor, parent, or adult. Discuss the beliefs about God, women, men, nonbinary people, sin, and other theological ideas in your prayer. Consider *theodicy* as not "a defense of God, but . . . wrestling with whether it is possible for God to exist, to be all-good, all-powerful, all-knowing, and for evil and suffering to exist as well."[20] An example of a prayer for youth pastors is below.

Gracious God, once again we gather in this space as your faithful servants. We praise you, adore you, and acknowledge you as the Triune God. We give you thanks for the gift of life since we last met together. Lord, we intend to learn from each other so that we can serve as effective youth pastors in our congregations. We come with questions and curiosities as well as our own cares and concerns. We come as sincere and steadfast servants trying to focus on our calling to this good work. Yet, even as we focus, we are distracted, like static on the radio when we search for a clear station. We hear static on the line when we try to connect to you, God. Some of us are distracted by the static of pain in our bodies, some by the suffering or loss of loved ones, and some by the static of evil in our jobs. Help us to push through the pain, suffering, and evil with hope that the static will be cleared up and we will be completely focused on you and the tasks before us. God, through the power of your Holy Spirit, we ask that you remind us that in your word in Romans 8:26 we read, "The Spirit helps us in our weakness; for we do not know how to pray as we ought, but that very Spirit intercedes with sighs too deep for words." Remind us that your Spirit is interceding for us daily. Thank you for bringing us this opportunity to serve through youth ministry. Most loving God, empower us to work through the static of suffering and evil to clearly hear your words of wisdom. In the name of the Creator—God, Redeemer—Jesus Christ, and Sustainer—the Holy Spirit. Amen.

Notes

1. Paulo Freire, *Pedagogy of the Oppressed*, 30th anniversary ed. (Continuum, 2003).
2. bell hooks, *Teaching to Transgress: Education as the Practice of Freedom* (Routledge, 1994).
3. Johnathan Jodamus, Megan Robertson, and Sarojini Nadar, "Transdisciplinary, Transgressive, and Transformative: Pedagogical Reflections on Sexual Ethics, Religion, and Gender," *Critical African Studies* (2022): 1–16.
4. Jodamus, Robertson, and Nadar, "Transdisciplinary, Transgressive, and Transformative," 5.
5. Elliot W. Eisner, *The Educational Imagination: On the Design and Evaluation of School Programs* (Macmillan, 1994).
6. "As Texas Revises Social Studies Curriculum, Residents Call for More Civics and New Courses," K-12 Dive, August 10, 2022, https://www.k12dive.com/news/as-texas-revises-social-studies-curriculum-residents-call-for-more-civics/629362/.
7. Maria Harris, *Fashion Me a People: Curriculum in the Church* (Westminster John Knox, 1989), 63.

8. K. C. Basile et al., "Interpersonal Violence Victimization Among High School Students—Youth Risk Behavior Survey, United States, 2019," *Morbidity and Mortality Weekly Report* supplements 69, no. 1 (2020): 28.

9. Religious leaders I interviewed in both Cape Town, West Africa, and the US agreed that teaching about teen dating violence worked better when it was an aspect of teaching about human sexuality.

10. Here I use Karen Tye's systematic concept of Christian education in her book *Basics of Christian Education* (Chalice, 2000) as a model for discussing human sexuality education. I am affirming the need to discuss a concept when thinking about education about gender-based violence with youth.

11. Kate M. Ott, *Sex + Faith: Talking with Your Child from Birth to Adolescence* (Westminster John Knox, 2013), 23.

12. Ott, *Sex + Faith*, 23.

13. Ott, *Sex + Faith*.

14. Tamar Kamionkowski, "Violence Against Women in the Hebrew Bible," The Shalvi/Hyman Encyclopedia of Jewish Women, August 1, 2023, https://jwa.org/encyclopedia/article/violence-against-women-in-the-hebrew-bible.

15. Kamionkowski, "Violence Against Women."

16. Alicia Tarrant, interview by author, July 10, 2023. Tarrant is the program coordinator for the Mississippi Gulf Coast Center for Nonviolence.

17. See David A. Kolb's experiential learning theory. One helpful resource is Colin Beard and John P. Wilson, *Experiential Learning: A Best Practice Handbook for Educators and Trainers*, 2nd ed. (Kogan Page, 2006). For a different approach to teaching, see multiple intelligence theory.

18. Augusto Boal, *Games for Actors and Non-Actors* (Routledge, 1992).

19. Centers for Disease Control, "Sexual Violence and Intimate Partner Violence Among People with Disabilities," April 23, 2024, https://www.cdc.gov/sexual-violence/about/sexual-violence-and-intimate-partner-violence-among-people-with-disabilities.html.

20. Almeda M. Wright, *The Spiritual Lives of Young African Americans* (Oxford University Press, 2017), 122.

CHAPTER TWO

Preaching Toward Teen Faith Formation

While preaching a sermon on 2 Samuel 13 about the rape of Tamar, "a faithful lady" in his congregation confronted Rev. Zukisa Fumba of the Belville South Methodist Society in the Cape Town suburb of Belville. "Reverend, no, it's not like that. These men right here are good men!" she insisted. She was responding to Fumba's admonishment of the men in the church and beyond as being part of the problem of gender-based violence, as being complicit with violence against girls and women. Fumba's response was, "I'm so grateful that I've evoked some [kind of a response]!" He spoke about the men being part of the problem. He encouraged them to speak out about gender-based violence to bring about change in practices and policies. He told the women, "Yes, you might have found a way for coping with it, but the problem [continues] to multiply."

Fumba is aware that more women than men in his congregation resist his preaching and teaching about gender-based violence, and that in general his congregation of "elite people, some of whom are professors," is uncomfortable with talking about gender-based violence in Bible study classes.[1] Nevertheless, Rev. Fumba teaches lessons on texts of terror and raises issues about gender and violence. He believes that gender-based violence is a violation of our humanity, regardless of the identity of a human being—female, male, homosexual, nonbinary, or heterosexual.

His passion to prevent and intervene in teen dating violence is fueled by seeing his father physically and psychologically violate and abuse his mother. Rev. Fumba has focused on gender-based violence as a leader in the Methodist Church of Southern Africa for more than ten years. In addition to serving the Belville South Methodist Church, in 2019 he was responsible for all youth work in the Methodist region of the Western Cape, which includes children in Sunday schools and older youth groups. He indicates that there are many youth in the Shona ethnic group who migrated with their parents from Zimbabwe to the Western Cape who are active in the Methodist Society. Some of the teenage girls in particular have talked about being sexually violated while participating in confirmation classes. This is what drives his preaching and his desire for resources about teen dating violence that can be used with youth not only in settings such as confirmation classes but also in congregational preaching.

Preaching by anyone who uses religious rhetoric can be instrumental in preventing and intervening in teen dating violence through faith and spiritual formation. Lisa Thompson, a womanist homiletics professor, highlights the ethics of preaching to audiences who inevitably include victims of gender-based violence, specifically teenagers, or those who live in fear of potential harm from a partner.[2] Thompson argues for trusting your own feelings and experiences of listening to sermons and how they affect you and others around you. The ethics of preaching about teen dating violence and how teens and their congregations feel about such sermons are inseparable in terms of preventing and intervening in teen dating violence. Thompson emphasizes concern to do no harm to victims or those who are at risk of teen dating violence. When the words of a preacher are received as truth, the antidote to a problem, fulfillment for those who are empty, and hope for those in despair, then those words become formative. These are some of the ways a sermon captures the mind and imagination of teens. The words of the preacher have power to affect the feelings, thoughts, and actions of teens. The preacher who intentionally foregrounds the possibility of trauma for teens in violent relationships is engaged in ethical preaching about teen dating violence.

At the same time, preaching about teen dating violence is also prophetic preaching. Neichelle Guidry, dean of Sisters Chapel at Spelman College, defines prophetic preaching as "the style of preaching that seeks to address social issues and articulate the social agenda of the church."[3] Guidry argues for prophetic preaching grounded in a womanist homiletical theology that subverts rape culture, in which Black women are dehumanized and demonized in the Black church and broader culture. Her focus on the sexual violence experienced by Black women and poor white women is relevant to the experiences of all teenage victims of sexual violence, regardless of race, gender, or sexual identity. Guidry's thesis is apropos to a campaign to end teen dating violence. Her position on prophetic preaching and preachers who are public theologians when they practice prophetic preaching suggests the formative nature of this form of preaching when focused on teen gender-based violence.

Preaching as Faith Formation for Youth

The formal moments in which clergy and youth pastors voice their interpretations of sacred texts to audiences of youth during worship or meditations shape the faith and spirituality of teens. As noted above, when the words of a preacher are received as truth, the antidote to a problem, fulfillment for those who are empty, and hope for those in despair, then those words become formative. The words of the preacher, undergirded by the preacher's authority and standing in the community, have the power to affect the feelings, thoughts, and actions of listeners, as they did for the woman who spoke up in resistance to Rev. Fumba's sermon about the rape of Tamar and the responsibility of men in the church to speak to other men about the problem of violence against women and girls. The preacher's words have power to form and to shape teens' behaviors.

The term *faith formation* refers to faith development in adolescents, which is particularly acute for youth when they are between eleven and twenty.[4] Shantelle Weber, a professor at Stellenbosch University in Cape Town, South Africa, considers the context of South African youth as she conceptualizes faith formation. Starting with a critique of James Fowler, who aligns with the development theory of Erik Erikson's psychosocial development of children, Lawrence Kohlberg's theory of moral development, and Jean Piaget's theory of cognitive development,[5] Weber argues that such biological development is an idea based on Eurocentric experiences. She speaks of spiritual/faith formation in this manner:

> Spiritual formation . . . is very connected to faith formation. . . . It's a lifelong process. It's not a stagnant process. It's an evolving process that is influenced by varying contextual and developmental realities. The only difference between faith and spiritual formation [is that] . . . I see faith as including my cognitive faith processes, my moral faith processes, and my identity [as a person of] faith process, whereas spiritual formation is about the identity. . . . In interfaith conversations spiritual is helpful because of the notion of spirituality is an easily defined term. These terms are all related to ecclesial discipleship.[6]

Faith formation for Weber is a lifelong process of cognitive faith, moral faith, and identity development circumscribed by a specific setting or a particular socioeconomic, sociocultural, sociohistorical, and sociopolitical context. Cognitive and moral faith formation as well as identity as a religious or spiritual person take place through relationships in the family and church.[7] "Faith becomes a set of beliefs and values the young person puts together from his or her interpretation of what has been taught, their life experiences, and their encounter with God."[8] The capacity to think about beliefs and values and to search for truth, adopt character traits, and practice making decisions that are congruent with values and beliefs is part of faith formation. Faith formation in youth requires various modes[9] and multiple programs, including reading sacred texts/Scripture, prayer, community service, worship, and fellowship. Preaching is a mode of faith formation with youth that requires thoughtful preparation, taking seriously various aspects of the listening congregation of both teenagers and adults, including psychosocial development and maturity. It is important to preach to a congregation about teen dating violence fully aware of and prepared for various responses to the sermon.

Encouraging better reception of preaching among teenagers in a congregation, especially on an unfamiliar topic such as teen dating violence, requires attention to the problem of marginalization of youth in the church and boring them during the sermon. It also requires nurturing a wholesome relationship between the preacher, preaching, and youth. Anna Carter Florence, preaching professor at Columbia Theological Seminary, addresses these concerns using Acts 20:7–12 to frame her position on preaching to teenagers.[10] The Acts text talks about a young man named Eutychus who began to sleep during Paul's long sermon. Eutychus was sitting in an open window on the third floor and fell to his death. This tragic event stopped Paul, who went down and held the young man until he revived.

While many interpretations focus of Paul's ability to resurrect Eutychus, Florence uses the text to make three points about preaching to teenagers. First, the young listener was literally bored to death. He was on the windowsill of the room, and his fall prompted a crisis. He was marginalized, and it was the church's preaching that put him at risk.[11] Second, marginalized teens, sitting on the edge of the congregation, suffer from the separation of youth ministry and preaching ministry. Rarely are teens asked about the sermon and how it might be relevant to their experiences. The topic and the language leave them feeling lost and ignorant, argues Florence.[12] Last, Florence admonishes preachers to "stop, look, listen, notice, ask, be open to conversation" with youth as a method of resurrecting sermons and youth.[13]

In addition to her three contextual concerns about preaching to teenagers, Florence stresses the importance of having a theology of youth ministry that is consistent with a practice of everyone in the congregation being gathered in worship together rather than holding separate worship services for teens apart from adult members of the congregation.[14] Florence's model prepares teens and their congregations to hear prophetic preaching against teen dating violence that can be transformative as well as formative of their faith.

A Personal Story of Faith Formation

My story of faith formation as a teenager through listening to preaching, although not through preaching about dating violence, illustrates what Weber posits above. The experience of hearing the preaching of Bishop Joseph A. Johnson Jr. and how it shaped my faith gives a glimpse of faith formation in a particular context that is different from what Florence discusses. My experience of hearing sermons as a teen during a religious training program illustrates how preaching can form the spirituality of a teenager.

I attended the Leadership Training School held each summer in Mississippi and sponsored by the Fourth Episcopal District of the Christian Methodist Episcopal Church. The Christian Methodist Episcopal training schools were youth camps held all over the United States primarily on college campuses owned by the Christian Methodist Episcopal Church. While I don't remember what we were trained to do in the classes I took, I remember how I felt when I sat in a class taught by someone I admired. I remember most vividly how I felt uplifted and affirmed as a Black teenager when I heard Bishop Joseph A. Johnson Jr. preach. It seemed as if I could taste, touch, smell, and feel every word he uttered. More significantly for me, he made my Blackness important. The tone of his voice made me imagine he was from a different land far beyond Mississippi and Louisiana people and their dialects that I was accustomed to hearing. His regal posture and the clothes that adorned his frame signified a proud Black preacher and bishop whom I claimed as my own.

Equally compelling was the way he taught us new words, new ideas, and new ways to think about familiar Scriptures. He challenged me and moved me to tears and to action beyond the worship service after hearing his sermons. He modeled academic excellence and prompted me to want to become an intellectual like him. Leadership Training School was a site for my formation as a Black teenage girl who could achieve anything because Bishop Johnson said I could. His embodiment of a Black liberation theology proclaimed that God was on the side of poor and oppressed Black people, such as me, my family, and members of my congregation. His preaching was a Black theology that I could hear, see, and emulate.

As a teenager growing up in southern Mississippi, the mantra "I'm Black and I'm proud!" popularized by the Rev. Jesse Jackson, pervaded my thinking. Bishop Johnson's preaching theologically baptized the popular saying among Black teens at the Leadership Training School, who were coming of age during the civil rights movement. His preaching transported my teenage mind to a realm of new possibilities and new promises, not only at the Leadership Training School but also at the National Youth Conference, which was the quadrennial youth event to which Christian Methodist Episcopal youth came from all over the world.

Bishop Johnson preached during the opening worship service during my first experience of a National Youth Conference in Birmingham, Alabama, on the campus of Miles College. I was sixteen years old. Youth from the Louisiana and Mississippi—Fourth Episcopal District left the recently segregated Tutwiler Hotel to arrive on the Miles College campus to secure front-row seats to hear and support our bishop, who was scheduled to preach the opening night of the conference. I gobbled down my barbecue meal, served on a paper plate, while sitting among hundreds of other teens on the lawn of what seemed like a huge campus. I was determined to have a good view of the bishop. Bishop Johnson preached the keynote address, titled "Beyond Blackness to Destiny." His sermon gave me a vision of life after desegregation and the Jim/Jane Crow policies and practices in Mississippi and surrounding southern regions with which I was familiar. Bishop Johnson's sermon was an experience of hope in a God who promised to end racial oppression in the United States. Thus, his sermon was an aspect of my early formation in the belief and practice of Christian hope.

When I was seventeen, I conceived and helped organize the first Christian Methodist Episcopal Meridian District Youth Festival, hosted by my own congregation, St. James Christian Methodist Episcopal Church. Our preacher was Bishop Johnson, who graciously agreed to come in response to the invitation I typed on my new electric typewriter, received upon graduating from high school in May 1970. I needed a blessing from Bishop Johnson to assuage my fear of going away from home alone for the first time to Lambuth College in Jackson, Tennessee. He did not disappoint me. In his sermon, titled "Taking a Trip with Jesus," he urged us not to succumb to psychedelic drugs and marijuana as we ventured into the new world of freedom on a college campus. The August 1970 youth festival and

Bishop Johnson's sermon were what I needed to be confident in leaving for college just two weeks later.

My mother, Geraldine F. Parker, took me to clean the homes of the sick, shut-in, and elderly. Faith formation was evidenced with our hands. She modeled spiritual formation through service to those less fortunate than our family. But I never heard her talk in protest and resistance about justice for women who were being abused, although she knew such women. I cannot recall social or religious critiques of sexism and patriarchy in the church or religious critiques of the violent abuse I witnessed in my community.

My mother, on the other hand, admonished me never to hesitate to tell her if any man or boy touched me inappropriately. My first memory of such wrongful touching was when a white man visited my great-aunt Maude's farm. I was about five years old. I don't remember the reasons for his visit. I only remember when he stood behind me with his hands pressing firmly on my shoulders, and then he moved them down my small frame to my vagina, as if measuring it with his hands. I squirmed away from him and told my mother about the incident later that evening. She told me to come to her immediately if that ever happened to me again. My mother made me feel protected, as if she would willingly sacrifice her own life and well-being to protect me from being sexually abused. She kept her promise of protection through subtle reminders throughout my teenage years as she gave me lessons on human sexuality that were sometimes embarrassing because she always called human body parts by their name—vagina and penis, for example—rather than nicknames such as pussycat and wee-wee. She gave me a sense of agency and confidence. She acted on her own agency as a mother and provided me with the tools to act if anyone ever groped me or touched me inappropriately. My education in sexuality came via homeschooling, and it included a component of gender-based violence education. Yet, my witness of gender-based violence in the community indicates that I observed the tormenting of tangible grace as I was being formed to think and act ethically as a person of faith.

While my experiences and learning of wrongful touch and gender-based violence came in my home, it would have been great if I had heard sermons about gender-based violence in my local church. The combination of teaching and preaching would have formed me by faith and spirituality in the way that Weber defines. If gender-based violence is talked about in the home, it becomes more normal to talk about it in church. Pastors can preach texts of terror and teenagers can connect with those sermons because they have had similar conversations at home.

The Experience of Torment During Preaching

How is the faith and spirituality of a teenager shaped when her body hurts during Sunday worship—a site of Christian faith formation—from the slaps and punches her partner has administered just hours before? Hearing a sermon is an opportunity to experience faith and spiritual formation that addresses the pain she feels from physical abuse the night before. The message from the sermon should be helpfully formative by offering theological and practical critical thinking about the preached word. Ethical values should permeate the sermon to help her make the best decisions about the worth of her body.

If a youth never hears a sermon or other proclamation about gender-based violence as part of their faith formation yet is at risk of experiencing gender-based violence, that teen will be likely to have destructive and unhealthy notions about love and relationships, and not know how to choose friends and lifelong partners. There can be an incongruence between lived experience and faith that comes through hearing the preached word if the sermon a young woman hears about violence against women fails to name the violence as abuse. Moreover, her faith formation will be delayed and distorted because of her experience of violence at the hands of her partner.

Likewise, imagine how a teenage, queer, cisgender boy feels when his boyfriend calls him stupid and a nobody just a few hours before they dance together during the last camp social and leaving for home the next morning. How does a boy cope after being raped the day before by the male camp counselor who preaches the sermon during the closing worship? His body, mind, and spirit are tormented by the incongruence of a violent assault to his body by a trusted adult in the religious context of a church camp. Listening to a preacher who raped him may be unbearable, or he may sit among the worshippers in a catatonic state, unable to respond, or he may even view the incident as an expression of love. These scenarios describe contexts where the faith of a teenager is formed, and preaching is a central activity in the formation of faith.

Perhaps the woman who stood up and spoke out to Fumba was a victim of years of abuse, and her body had been tormented so long that she had become compliant with male abuse and domination. Perhaps she was in denial. Perhaps she had never had any experiences of gender-based violence with the men in the church or anywhere else. But there were teenage girls and boys sitting in the congregation who also reacted to Fumba's sermon when she resisted. Their possible reaction leads us to ask: What were their experiences? What were they thinking when they heard the biblical text about the rape of Tamar by her half-brother? What did they feel about the text? The story? What questions lay within them that yearned to be spoken?

Preaching to youth forms the moral and spiritual life of teenagers. In such situations, preachers must attend to teens' context, particularly to the possibility that gender-based violence is already tormenting their bodies and spirits and that their existing trauma will affect how they receive or hear the formative aspects of the sermon. Questions to considered include: What are the ethics of communicating sacred rhetoric to queer and straight teens about gender-based violence? What process for sacred communication or sacred meaning-making with young women might prevent or intervene in violence in their romantic relationships? What is an ethic of communicating to young women and young, queer, cisgender males in religious contexts? An ethic of religious and sacred communication that generates mindful, accountable meaning-making must be a priority in preaching for faith formation with youth. These questions and the ones above are central to the process of faith formation through sermons teens hear about teen dating violence.

Preaching Practices for Prevention and Intervention

Preaching in a religious setting with youth should be truthful and just, generating wholesome, sacred meaning-making. Consider the ethics of communicating to and caring for trans- and cisgender youth who have experienced violence in their romantic relationships. Partner violence is an issue that is central to sacred rhetoric or preaching in order to intervene in gender-based violence among young people. There are three practices to consider when preaching to youth to prevent and intervene in teen dating violence: evoking feelings, educating toward enlightenment, and empowering sound decision-making.

Evoke a Range of Feelings

First, use your sermon deliberately to evoke the passionate feelings of youth who are listening. Other than regular Sunday gatherings, consider that church camps and youth revivals are two of several highly charged emotional settings in which your youth might be immersed. Seize the opportunity to prompt feelings about the issue of gender-based violence. Anticipate feelings to erupt and interrupt your sermon. At the same time, be prepared to give pastoral care to those whose feelings are a response to trauma they have experienced (for more on pastoral care in response to gender-based violence, see chapter 4).

Likewise, anticipate other responses too. For example, instead of assuming that young women experiencing a sermon around a text of terror are victims or survivors feeling anxious or uncomfortable about the sermon and the memories it has evoked, consider that they might instead feel emboldened to act to counter such violence and the patriarchy and sexism that reinforce the "idea of oppression, superiority, and even punishment [as being] from God."[15] Thompson says, "We [women] are prone to have our voices suppressed. Part of the process [of preaching] is to help people recover their questions that lie dormant within them. The role of the sermon is to help those questions bubble up again."[16] Consider these steps for evoking feelings and stimulating dormant questions in youth.[17] Invite youth to

1. Read the text. As a component of preaching preparation, invite youth to list feelings that surface from reading the text on which you will be preaching.
2. Give experiences of the text. Ask youth to list their experiences but at this point don't ask them to interpret the text or justify or analyze the feelings that surface.
3. List the questions that have been lingering about the text as well as list new questions. It is important to help people recover the questions that they already have, even if at present those questions are dormant within them.

Educate Toward Enlightenment

Educating toward enlightenment means preaching to make youth aware of the problem of gender-based violence. The sermon should inspire a hunger in the youth to learn more about what they are hearing and feeling. The sermon should move the youth to develop "the capacity for critical consciousness or critical thinking."[18] Central to critical thinking is freeing youth to ask questions that have been forbidden or silenced in worship, church school, youth group, and other religious settings where youth congregate.

The preacher should facilitate a space to practice educating for enlightenment, which can be the same space for discussing feelings. Enlightenment helps youth practice critical theological questioning.[19] Two resources to help raise consciousness about intimate-partner violence are movies and music lyrics.[20] These familiar forms of popular culture stimulate discussion. For example, introduce and define the term *misogyny* (namely, individual prejudice or hatred of women and girls, as well as institutional and ingrained hatred of women and girls) and other, related terms. Then, explain how movies and music lyrics promote misogynistic behavior. If parents permit, include in your discussions movies and music lyrics that are explicitly homophobic, chauvinistic, and predatory. Invite the youth to compile a list of such movies and music. My list of movies would include *The Wolf of Wall Street*, where women and girls are objectified and treated as disposable objects, only useful for sex, along with *The Devil Wears Prada*, *Thirteen*, and *Pariah*. Music videos provide limitless music-and-movie combinations for analysis and raising critical theological questions.

After showing the movie or music video, facilitate discussion to help the youth become enlightened about gender-based violence. Ask questions that (1) help youth become enlightened about how they are represented in movies and music videos. How are the main characters portrayed? What stereotypes obviously refer to you or those you know? What do the stereotypes imply about the worth of youth and those youth know?[21] Then ask questions that (2) help youth become enlightened about the ways in which they might be on the margin or at the center of community and the greater society. Who is popular in your setting? Who is not? Who decides? Who is silenced? Who is given voice? Who has the power to silence and give voice? How is silencing someone related to gender-based violence? What are the power dynamics of gender-based violence? What are some others?

Empower Sound Decision-Making

Preaching should empower teenagers to make decisions about their bodies—their God-given gift of tangible grace—and how their bodies will be treated in their relationships. The decisions that teenagers make should bring joy and keep them safe even when all around them—their schools, communities, governments—seem to fail at maintaining their happiness and safety. When a preacher is clear about the purpose of the preached word for congregations including teenagers—whose minds can reason and think abstractly, although they are not fully mature—then they can proclaim a word from God that will empower teens to make choices yielding joy and safety in their lives. There are primarily three aspects of empowering teens to make sound decisions.

1. The sermon should provide a clear pathway or process to the many choices or options from which a teen must choose each day.
2. The sermon should give a teen agency, that is, power to act in a manner that is life giving for themselves and others.
3. The sermon should give a teenager confidence that God, present in the Holy Spirit who dwells within them, will guide their thoughts and actions.

In addition to empowering youth to make sound decisions, empower them to be central to shaping the content and best ways to preach about teen dating violence in all sermons. Use Florence's practice when teaching her course Preaching and Youth, asking teenagers:[22]

- What is the most important part of worship for adults?
- What is the most important part of worship for youth?
- What are your suggestions for worship and preaching in your congregation? What topics, passages of Scripture?
- How would you like to participate in the sermon preparation and delivery?
- How can you lead other teens in preparation to preach and hear the sermon?

Also consider how you can empower teens to participate in a youth preaching camp or create and host a preaching camp for teens in their region.[23] The above practices of evoking, enlightening, and empowering teenagers through preaching have the potential for wholesome faith formation among teens.

Notes

1. While Rev. Zukisa Fumba did not mention the reaction of teenagers in his congregation to his preaching about gender-based violence, he is committed to ending teen dating violence through his ministry with them.
2. Rev. Lisa Thompson, interview by author, July 1, 2023.
3. Neichelle R. Guidry, "Towards a Womanist Homiletical Theology for Subverting Rape Culture" (PhD diss., Garrett Evangelical Theological Seminary, 2017), vi.
4. Steve Emery-Wright and Ed Mackenzie, *Networks for Faith Formation: Relational Bonds and the Spiritual Growth of Youth* (Wipf & Stock, 2017), xvi–xvii.
5. These theorists have been foundational in terms of the psychosocial, moral, and cognitive development of children. Many primary and secondary sources are available for further reading.
6. Shantelle Weber, interview by author, July 20, 2023.
7. Shantelle Weber, "Faith Formation of Young People in an Evangelical Context: An Empirical and Theoretical Investigation" (PhD diss., Stellenbosch University, 2014).
8. Weber, "Faith Formation of Young People," 239–40.
9. Weber, "Faith Formation of Young People," ch. 3.
10. Anna Carter Florence, "A Prodigal Preaching Story and Bored-to-Death Youth," *ThTo* 64, no. 2 (2007): 233–43, https://doi.org/10.1177/004057360706400208.

11. Florence, "Prodigal Preaching Story," 236.
12. Florence, "Prodigal Preaching Story," 239.
13. Florence, "Prodigal Preaching Story," 242.
14. I discuss the practice of asking teens to evaluate sermons with the preacher in the section on practices, which is similar to Florence's model. I also include her model as another alternative.
15. Thompson, interview.
16. Thompson, interview.
17. These steps are adapted from Thompson, interview.
18. Evelyn L. Parker, "Conclusion: Nurturing the Sacred Selves of Adolescent Girls," in *The Sacred Selves of Adolescent Girls: Hard Stories of Race, Class, and Gender*, ed. Evelyn L. Parker (Pilgrim, 2006), 166.
19. Parker, "Conclusion," 168.
20. Parker, "Conclusion," 165–70. The practices for critical theological questioning are modeled on those found in the section on realization in *Sacred Selves*.
21. Parker, "Conclusion." This list of questions is adapted from *Sacred Selves*.
22. Florence, "Prodigal Preaching Story," 237. I have added questions 4–5.
23. The youth preaching camp is based on the Academy of Preachers, founded in 2009 to inspire young people in the art and practice of gospel preaching. It is now housed at Belmont University in Nashville. See Academy of Preachers, https://www.academyofpreachers.net.

CHAPTER THREE

Liturgy and Worship as Pathways Toward Renewal

The Parcel

The parcel she went to collect
the one that took her life
and broke my heart

The one I packed with
Joy-filled things
to show her how much I miss her
and how well I know
the things she loves
just as was she

The one I loved
the moment she was
wrapped in sacred secret love
within my womb
as only a mother understands
and sends into the world

Only to be snatched
one cold stark day,
caught and robbed
torn open, broken, battered,
emptied, cast aside
by a man from whom
she went to fetch
the parcel of my love—
who stole the parcel of my love.[1]

St. Margaret's Anglican Church in Parow, a suburb of Cape Town, South Africa, is a place where teens participate with their families and serve as acolytes. St. Margaret's was my regular place of worship, my home church while away from home, during the six months that I did research for this book. The rector read "The Parcel" during a worship service at St. Margaret's. The church was also the community of faith where the Eucharist took on a more significant meaning for me. St. Margaret's hosted a worship service that remembered women and girls who had been violently killed in August and September 2019. Sarojini Nadar, director of the Desmond Tutu Centre for Religion and Social Justice at the University of the Western Cape (UWC), described the events of that time:

> September 2019 was dubbed the "September of Sorrow," in South Africa—a month in which the country shook as gender-based violence attack after attack came to light—A man murdered his wife after a marriage counselling session; a 25-year-old boxing champion was shot dead by her ex-boyfriend who was a police officer; a 19-year-old student at the University of Cape Town, Uyinene Mrwetayana, went to fetch a parcel from her local post office, where she was raped and bludgeoned to death by a post office worker. Not even a week later, an 18-year-old 1st-year student, registered in the department of Religion and Theology at the University of the Western Cape, Jesse Hess, was found raped and murdered next to her 85-year-old grandfather who was also murdered in their home. Indeed, the country was in mourning and in deep sorrow.[2]

As a Fulbright scholar, I participated in the life of the UWC community, including a memorial service for Hess that was held in the UWC auditorium and filled beyond capacity. The occasion included liturgical components of dramatic poetry, prose, testimonies, and passionate singing led by the UWC choir. The choir led us in singing "Ukuthula," a Zulu song of peace, which is often sung on many occasions, including memorial services. The words declare the peace and victory that Jesus brings in the world. The memorial service weaved interfaith liturgies, prayers and songs that celebrated Hess's life and offered a lasting image of human bodies, God's tangible grace, grieving, lamenting, and calling for justice against gender-based violence. Worship at St. Margaret's and the Jesse Hess memorial service convinced me that worship can be formative and can inspire teens to act for justice against dating violence too.

Faith Formation in Worship

Faith formation is a lifelong process of cognitive and moral faith and identity development circumscribed by a specific setting or a particular socioeconomic, sociocultural, sociohistorical, and sociopolitical context. Cognitive and moral faith formation as well as religious identity takes place through relationships primarily in the family and a Christian congregation.[3] Faith formation understood in this manner is synonymous with teenage spiritual formation.[4] Christian faith and spiritual formation of teenagers can motivate them to think and act justly in all sorts of situations, including cases of gender-based violence.

Christian believers espouse spiritual formation as "a process of becoming like Christ."[5] As Carmichael Crutchfield says, "The Holy Spirit is the active agent in the formation process."[6] God, through the power of the Holy Spirit, forms us in the image and likeness of Christ. The defining aspect of being formed in the image of Christ is our love of God, others, and self. Jesus taught this important commandment when he addressed the Pharisees, "'You shall love the Lord your God with all your heart, and with all your soul, and with all your mind.' This is the greatest and first commandment. And a second is like it: 'You shall love your neighbor as yourself'" (Matt 22:37–39). Love of God and love of others is made possible in us through the Holy Spirit, whom Jesus promised to be with us forever (John 14:15–16).

Additionally, Christian spiritual formation focuses on God's work in our lives through the gift of faith.[7] We have a reciprocal relationship with God. This relationship leads us to trust God, the keeper of promises, the steadfast lover of our souls.[8] Love is the essence of the reciprocal relationship with God. We love God, and God responds by loving us back. Paul in Romans 8:38–39 reminds us concerning God's love for us "that neither, death, nor life, nor angels, nor rulers, nor things present, nor things to come, nor powers, nor height, nor depth, nor anything else in all creation, will be able to separate us from the love of God in Christ Jesus our Lord."

We express our love for God through love of humankind, the earth, and all creation. Wedded to love is the act of justice, which we show to our neighbors, the earth, and all creatures. Our gracious God shows us love and justice through the life and practices of Jesus Christ. In response, we are required to give love and act justly. The prophet Micah reminds Israel that God does not require elaborate acts and expressions in worship to express gratitude. Micah asks in 6:8, "What does the LORD require of you but to do justice, and to love kindness, and to walk humbly with your God?" Loving God requires doing justice, and God reciprocates love and justice to us. Likewise, Jesus Christ modeled love and justice throughout his life and ministry. He promised us the Holy Spirit to remind us and nudge us toward love and justice in our daily lives. We also express our love to God and acts of justice through worship, and God reciprocates love in the worship experience. Love of the Triune God and love of others is concretized in the words and rituals of the Christian worship experience, where the congregation gathers to adore and praise God.

Worship is among those expressions and practices of faith that parents and faith communities encourage for the faith and spiritual formation of teens. Whether Protestant or Catholic, youth are formed in the Christian faith when they experience the reading of sacred texts and hearing prayers, chanting, and singing in worship. As Crutchfield says, "Participation in Christian worship is an expression and renewal of Christian service as an act of faith."[9] Aspects of Christian worship include celebration of the sacraments, prayer, reading and hearing Scripture, and engaging in fellowship. Music as a form of worshipping God is also significant for faith formation of youth,[10] as is liturgical dance. These modes of worship position teens to be drawn into a relationship with God, known in Jesus Christ and active in the world as the Holy Spirit.

Crutchfield writes, "Worship is not only the most important congregational event, but it also presents the greatest opportunity for faith formation."[11] Songs, prayers, litanies, chants, rituals, and all other aspects of worship "nurture a relationship of trust with God and form or shape the way we see God, ourselves, and the world."[12] Recalling formative experiences of worship while he was coming of age in Barrs Chapel Christian Methodist Episcopal Church in Como, Tennessee, Crutchfield tells of singing the hymn "Holy, Holy, Holy," every Sunday. The words "Holy, holy, holy, Lord God Almighty," and "God in three Persons, blessed Trinity" formed his theological belief in and solidified his adoration of the Trinity. He concludes, "Worship forms our faith, our love relationship with the triune God."[13]

His account of formation in worship through singing prompts me to think about my own spiritual formation as a teenager through singing in worship. Worship was the context where love of the Triune God became real and accessible to me. When we sang through call-and-response the "Old One Hundred" song, led by J. C. Fairley, "I love the Lord, He heard my cry," I experienced the love of God and the demand for justice amid struggle and despair while coming of age in Hattiesburg,

Mississippi, a key site of the civil rights movement during the 1960s. I also grew up singing the hymn "Jesus Loves Me." This song was a staple on Sundays when the youth or children's choir sang in worship. Among the hymns that I learned to play on the piano was "They'll Know We Are Christians." This hymn gave me a feeling of comfort in the community of Christians who acted and behaved in ways that were inconsistent with the teachings of Jesus Christ. I would play and sing, "We are one in the Spirit, we are one in the Lord. . . . Yes, they will know we are Christians by our love."[14] While I don't recall playing this hymn for the St. James Christian Methodist Episcopal Church youth choir, I loved the words and the melody so much that I'm sure I played it as a backdrop for altar call and prayer time during worship services. Like Crutchfield's, my faith in the Triune God was shaped by the theology of hymns sung in worship.

The Experience of Torment in a Worship Community

When worship is among the settings where teens develop a relationship with the Triune God, they are empowered to do amazing things, including denouncing teen dating violence. However, the teenager who has a relationship with God, known in Jesus Christ, whose Spirit dwells in the body of a teen, still may be tormented by a violent romantic relationship. There is irony in the fact that a teenager who participates regularly in worship as a liturgist, usher, greeter, or acolyte also can experience physical or psychological violence from a partner. This is indicative of tormented tangible grace in worship, which happens more than some are willing to admit.

In January 2018, during a youth ministry conference, a youth pastor pulled me aside after my lecture on teen dating violence and asked for help with a situation in his youth ministry. A teenage girl in his youth group confided in him that she was being repeatedly raped by a teenage boy who was also a member of the youth group. Although this was not a dating relationship, it's easy to perceive that such a scenario might exist. She was desperate for help because she had told her parents, but they didn't believe her because the teenage boy was the son of her family's close friends. The youth pastor did not know what to do about the situation as he kept her secret with hopes to find a solution. In the meantime, both teens were simultaneously worshipping in their congregation. Imagine the torment she felt within her body each time she saw her abuser in worship as well as in the youth group. No doubt scenes of his abusive acts flooded her mind as she saw him singing, praying, and leading the congregation in a responsive reading.

I reminded the youth pastor of his legal responsibility to report this situation to the authorities. Also, I suggested that he find a way to convene a conversation with the parents of these teenagers with the support of his senior pastor. Surely, the indwelling Holy Spirit of the victim was also suffering just as the teenage victim of sexual assault was suffering. We know that the Holy Spirit, in conjunction with our spirit, helps us when we are tormented. The Spirit, writes Paul to the Romans, "helps us in our weakness," for the rape victim does not know how to pray for relief from the egregious violation of a sexual assault, "but that very Spirit intercedes with sighs too deep for words" (8:26). "And God . . . knows what is the mind of the Spirit" (8:27). There is comfort in knowing that the Holy Spirit has the power to assuage the tormented tangible grace of the teenage victim of sexual assault even as she worships as well as to urge repentance of the abuser in worship, both in the same worshipping congregation.

Rituals as Prevention and Intervention

Christian congregations use rituals in worship to help form the faith of their youth. These rituals can be as informal as a youth pastor blessing teens by the laying on of hands every time they gather. Or the ritual can be as intentional as the celebration of confirmands on Confirmation Sunday in the Christian tradition. Rituals are a significant part of worship and help shape the spirituality of a teenager.

The Eucharist, as a ritual in Christian worship, can help transform the tormenting of teens' tangible grace for perpetrators and survivors. Eucharist is a powerful sacrament.[15] Eucharist, also called Holy Communion or the Lord's Supper in some traditions, is the ritual reenactment of Jesus taking bread and wine after supper during his last meal with his disciples before his crucifixion. Paul refers to this meal as the supper of the Lord in 1 Corinthians 11:20–25.[16] It evolved from a common meal in which Jesus spoke words that have become the words of institution, found in 1 Corinthians 11:23b–26.[17] It's a ritualized religious ceremony blessed by the power of the Holy Spirit, which transcends secular or human understanding.

The Eucharist or Holy Communion includes movement, receiving the elements, the posture of those receiving the elements, a spoken liturgy, and the liturgical attire of the celebrants or liturgists. All the senses of the human body experience these components. Some Christian traditions, such as the Orthodox Church and Catholic Church, allow only members to celebrate the Eucharist. The Christian Methodist Episcopal Church and many other Protestant denominations welcome all people, including children, teenagers, the baptized and unbaptized, members and visitors, to partake of Holy Communion. All can freely choose to participate in the holy sacrament. No one is compelled to receive the bread and the wine. However, some Christian Methodist Episcopal congregations continue to use liturgy that admonishes repentance of sins.

At St. Margaret's Anglican Church, songs, hymns, litanies, prayers, the passing of the peace, Eucharist, and other components were integrated into worship. The ritual of confirmation of St. Margaret's youth was one such added component to the worship service. In the Anglican Church tradition this rite is performed after the youth has been baptized, usually as a baby but also anytime afterward, and makes a commitment to the faith.[18] The bishop of the Anglican Church lays hands on each teen, prays for them, and anoints each one of them as a sign of increased gifting of the Holy Spirit. In preparation for the rite of confirmation, the teens participate in educational settings where they learn the history, doctrines, rituals, and practices of the church. These formal educational settings are formational for teens. Yet, for some there is the fear that teens will estrange themselves from the church after confirmation. While there is anecdotal evidence that some youth become uninterested in the church after confirmation, the spiritual formation of acolytes, who were always teenagers at St. Margaret's, took place primarily through their duties and responsibilities during worship. Acolytes processed into the sanctuary with the clergy, holding the Bible, the cross, and incense. They also assisted the celebrant of Holy Communion. At the end of the service, they processed out of the sanctuary carrying Christian symbols of the faith. These choreographed movements in worship were formational.

At St. Margaret's, teens who were not acolytes and chose to attend youth church joined the adults in worship just prior to the sacrament of Holy Communion each Sunday, following their separate youth worship service. Celebrating Communion intergenerationally is essential for wholesome Christian faith formation of teens. Communion on a regular basis allows teens to practice the ritual with all their senses as well as hear the prayers and hymns of the service. Communion is a full-body experience where the mind of a teen makes meaning of the liturgy in concert with the memory of the body during the ritual. When teens, along with significant adults in their lives, participate in the Lord's Supper, the Holy Spirit through the power of God strengthens the faith of a teen. Communion, partaking of the bread and wine, in the context of a worship service that focuses on teen dating violence would be formative for teens attending such a worship service.

Service of Hope amid Teen Dating Violence

Here is an example of a worship service of hope that includes the Eucharist for those tormented by teen dating violence.[19]

> **Gathering and Preparation:** The people of God gather to worship as they hear the church bell or the amplified music. They prepare to worship by receiving a bulletin that contains the name and picture of a person who has been killed by a rapist or a senseless act of femicide. Ushers instruct the congregants to pray for enlightenment in the worship service after reading the brief bio on the flip side of the picture.
>
> **Greetings:** Facing the congregation, the worship leader or liturgist greets the people and engages them with a responsive reading. This signals active participation with voice and movement of the body in the worship service from start to finish.
>
> > Bless the Lord, O my soul!
> > **And all that is within me, bless God's holy name!**
> > Bless the Lord, O my soul!
> > **Give thanks to God for God's love and mercy that shall never end!**
>
> **Hymn of Praise:** The choir leads the congregation in singing an upbeat hymn that gives praise and adoration to the Triune God for God's love and faithfulness to all God's people, a hymn such as "O God, Our Help in Ages Past" or "Come, We That Love the Lord/We're Marching to Zion."
>
> **Affirmation of Faith:** The Apostles' Creed is familiar and used most often in Protestant churches. However, there are other options from other Christian traditions, such as the ecumenical version of the Apostles' Creed:

Liturgist: Let us unite in confession of our Christian faith:

Liturgist and People: I believe in God the Father Almighty, creator of heaven and earth.

> I believe in Jesus Christ, his only son, our Lord, who was conceived by the Holy Spirit, born of the Virgin Mary, suffered under Pontius Pilate, was crucified, died, and was buried; he descended to the dead. On the third day he rose again; he ascended into heaven, is seated at the right hand of the Father, and will come again to judge the living and the dead.
> I believe in the Holy Spirit, the holy catholic church, the communion of saints, the forgiveness of sins, the resurrection of the body, and the life everlasting. Amen.

Opening Prayer: The worship leader invites the congregation to remain standing for prayer as they continue to commune with God and each other. This prayer may be extemporaneous or a printed prayer and spoken in unison by the people. The congregation can pray the following collect after the liturgist says, "Let us pray together:"

> O God, our Mother and Father, we are your children, our bodies created by your hands in your likeness, fashioned in your love.
> Be with us as we remember it was you who formed our inward parts, it was you who knit us together in our mother's wombs.
> Be with us as we celebrate you and give thanks for making us fearful and beautiful manifestations of your divine *agape*.
> Help us to appreciate and celebrate each other. We are all wonderful works of your unending love. Amen.

The congregation sits.

Prayer for Illumination: The liturgist prays a brief prayer for illumination before the Scripture readings. This prayer invokes the blessings of the Holy Spirit on the reading, preaching, and doing of God's holy word. The poetic lyrics of the hymn "O

Living Breath of God" can be read as the prayer or sung by the choir and congregation.[20]

> O living Breath of God, wind at the beginning upon the
>   waters;
> O living Breath of God, bearing the creation to wondrous
>   birth;
>
> O living Breath of God, by whose pow'r the Son came to
>   birth among us;
> O living Breath of God, who to the creation gives life
>   anew;
>
> O living Breath of God, bearing us to life through baptis-
>   mal waters;
> O living Breath of God, sighing with creation for free-
>   dom's birth;
>
> Come now, and fill our spirits; pour out your gifts
>   abundant.
> O living Breath of God, Holy Spirit, breathe in us as
>   we pray.
> Amen.

Scripture: The Scripture following the collect should reinforce the idea of God's creation of our bodies. It is also important to indicate a transition to a lament for battered, beaten bodies of intimate partners. Stories of rape in the Bible raise our awareness about rape in sacred texts. An Old Testament reading or a psalm is appropriate. Consider Genesis 1:26–27 or Genesis 2:7, 18–24. Consider reading stories of rape in the Hebrew Scriptures, including Genesis 19:30–38, Genesis 34:1–7, or 2 Samuel 13:1–22. Psalm 139:1–18 and Lamentations 3:19–30 are also possible readings.

Following the reading from the Old Testament:

> **Leader:** The Word of God for such a time as this.
> **Congregational Response: Thanks be to God. Amen**

The New Testament reading may be selected from the Gospels or any other Scripture that expresses hope in the Triune God. Suggestions include John 8:1–11 or Romans 8.

Following the reading from the New Testament:

> **Leader:** The Word of God for such a time as this.
> **Congregational Response: Thanks be to God. Amen**

Testimony in Liturgical Dance or Spoken Words: Instead of a sermon, consider including a liturgical dance choreographed in response to reading or study of Judges 19:22–30 (the Levite's concubine). The movements should evoke remorse, sorrow, and even repentance and pardon for the horrific and brutal killing of a woman, the total objectification and destruction of a partner. While the dance encompasses the entire passage of Judges 19, the reading before the sacred dance is Judges 19:22–30.

Another option for testimony is a mime of Judges 19, with only 19:22–30 spoken. Use an instrumental musical selection to transition from the dance or mime to spoken testimonies. Transition from the choreography of a dance or mime to three to five short testimonies from those who have been freed from situations of violence in a romantic relationship. Use the refrain from the musical selection to transition between each testimony.

Affirmations and Reponses to the Word: The worship leader invites the congregation to pray silently. Afterward, the liturgist offers a prayer of response to the word, such as the following:

O God, we know you feel the pain of rape, physical beatings, and emotional abuse by the hands of an intimate partner and even an unknown rapist. Heal those wounds. Give justice to the victims. Help us to continue to become aware of gender-based violence. Give us courage to comfort and protect those who are vulnerable and at risk of violence by a partner, especially youth. Give us courage to act justly as a result of our awareness. **Amen.**

Eucharist or Holy Communion: Follow the tradition of the congregation with the liturgy for Eucharist or Holy Communion. Be sure that the liturgy includes or is preceded by confession, pardon, and sharing the peace. Singing during the sharing of bread and wine is also important. Communion can also be customized specifically for a focus on gender-based violence.

Hymn of Hope: A hymn of hope sung by the congregation is appropriate after Communion. Suggestions include "Thank You, Lord"[21] and "Now Thank We All Our God."

Prayers for Hope and Wholeness, and Laying on of Hands: The worship leader announces the ceremony and gives instructions. Arrange stations for the laying on of hands in front of the congregation. There can be two people at each station. Both persons lay hands as one says, "Know that God is with you always."

Prayer After the Laying on of Hands:

> Almighty God, we pray that all who suffer from gender-based violence may be comforted in their suffering and made whole.
> When they are afraid, give them courage;
> when they feel weak, grant them your strength;
> when they are afflicted, afford them comfort;
> when they are lost, offer them hope;
> when they are alone, move us to their side;
> when death threatens their lives, empower us to act swiftly to save.
> In the name of Jesus Christ we pray. **Amen.**[22]

Hymn: A sending-forth hymn of hope for the end of gender-based violence. Suggestions include "I Know Who Holds Tomorrow,"[23] "My Faith Looks Up to Thee," and "His Eye Is on the Sparrow."

Dismissal with Blessing:

> The Triune God who intervenes in gender-based violence bless and keep you;
> The face of the Lord who prevents and protects teenagers from battering and beatings shine upon you and be gracious to you;
> the light of the countenance of the Lord who redeems your life be lifted upon you and give you peace. **Amen.**

Going Forth: Triumphant music as the congregation sits or moves out of the sanctuary. A reprise or medley of songs from earlier in the worship is appropriate.

Notes

1. Chris Ahrends, *Sacred Awakening: Lessons on the Path, Poems, Essay and Illustrations* (Print On Demand, Cape Town, South Africa, 2021), 45.

2. Sarojini Nadar, "Foreword," in *2019 Annual Report of the Desmond Tutu Centre for Religion and Social Justice* (Desmond Tutu Centre for Religion and Social Justice, 2019), 4. My research for this book was hosted by Professor Nadar and the Desmond Tutu Centre at the University of the Western Cape.

3. Weber, "Faith Formation of Young People."

4. Weber, "Faith Formation of Young People."

5. Carmichael Crutchfield, *The Formation of a People: Christian Education and the African American Church* (Judson, 2020), 42.

6. Crutchfield, *Formation of a People*, 43.

7. Crutchfield, *Formation of a People*, 44.

8. Crutchfield, *Formation of a People*, 45.

9. Crutchfield, *Formation of a People*, 45.

10. Crutchfield, *Formation of a People*, 45.

11. Crutchfield, *Formation of a People*, 79.

12. Crutchfield, *Formation of a People*, 80.

13. Crutchfield, *Formation of a People*, 80.

14. "They'll Know We Are Christians," by Peter Scholtes, © 1966, F.E.L. Publications, assigned to The Lorenz Corp., 1991.

15. Not all rituals that celebrate Eucharist or Holy Communion are the same. I have leaned heavily on the Eucharist in the Wesleyan tradition.

16. "Lord's Supper, the," in *Harper's Bible Dictionary*, gen. ed. Paul J. Achtemeier (Harper & Row, 1985), 576.

17. "Lord's Supper," 576.

18. Not all Protestant churches practice confirmation of youth. However, this ritual is an essential part of spiritual formation for Anglican teenagers.

19. The content of the Service of Hope is adapted from *The United Methodist Book of Worship* (United Methodist Publishing House, 1992). The outline format is adapted from Crutchfield, *Formation of a People*, ch. 7.

20. Osvaldo Catena, "O Living Breath of God," trans. Gerhard M. Cartfod, in *Evangelical Lutheran Worship* (Augsburg Fortress, 2006), 407.

21. "Thank You, Lord," in *African American Heritage Hymnal* (GIA, 2001), #531.

22. This prayer is modified from the prayer for anointing and laying on of hands from *United Methodist Book of Worship*, 621.

23. "I Know Who Holds Tomorrow," in *African American Heritage Hymnal*, #415.

CHAPTER FOUR

Pastoral Care as Relational Healing

Rev. Andy Stoker encountered a nineteen-year-old and an eighteen-year-old who wanted to get married in his church. Part of his process is to engage each couple in at least three pastoral conversations prior to their wedding. In working with the couple, it became clear that the male partner was, at the very least, emotionally abusing the female partner.

Stoker explored how each partner had seen conflict arise and dealt with in their family of origin. In the course of the conversations, he decided not to officiate their wedding because something about the couple was awry. He also asked them to speak with a different pastor of the same church to continue the counseling conversations before their wedding, noting that there was plenty of time to do so before the planned wedding date.

The couple, however, did not seek out another minister on the church staff and returned to Stoker for another session in which they tried to clean up whatever indication was there to merit a different minister for counseling and presiding over their marriage ceremony. The male partner mostly dominated that conversation. Stoker asked him to leave the room and for the female to stay with him for a few more minutes, assuring her that his administrative assistant was right outside his office and would attend to her partner as he waited. She did stay and indicated that her partner was indeed mentally and emotionally violent, and there had been a hint of potential physical violence. Afterward, Stoker invited the male partner back into the room and noted his pastoral relationship with the couple since they chose to return. Turning to the male partner, Stoker repeated that the couple needed counseling from a staff minister so that he could avoid what he felt was a potential conflict of interest as their pastor. Stoker said the male partner responded by pounding on the table and uttering a slew of cuss words. He then walked out, taking the young woman with him.

Six months later, the young woman made an appointment with Stoker, at which time she told him that a violent episode had indeed followed their last visit and that her partner had hit her. She had removed herself from the situation and was now following up with Stoker. She told Stoker that if it hadn't been for his giving her permission to talk about her relationship, she wouldn't have had the courage to recognize the problem and see the violent situation for what it was. "She said it was young love."[1] Rev. Stroker's philosophy on pastoral counseling intervention set limits on his own willingness to perform the couple's marriage. Equally important, those conversations revealed a violent and potentially deadly intimate relationship between a young engaged couple. That revelation came when touching that was once an expression of young love became touching that hurt.

Tormented Touch and Trauma

The role of pastoral care is to offer healing for those who have been traumatized by inappropriate touching as well as implement plans for prevention and intervention. Stephanie Crumpton, associate professor of practical theology at McCormick Theological Seminary, offers two practices of pastoral care for healing trauma from inappropriate touching for African-descended women that can be applicable for teens of all races and ethnicities who have been traumatized by inappropriate touching.[2] First, Crumpton urges pastoral caregivers to "become aware of cultural transference" when working with Black females. "Cultural countertransference means the deeply held, unconsciously motivated leanings about race, sexuality, class, ethnicity, gender and various other physical markers of social location that often result in stereotypes about Black women."[3] If we add age or ageism to Crumpton's list of unconscious motivated biases, such as stereotypes we may have about a teenager, cultural countertransference is relevant to the pastoral care practice of teens traumatized by dating violence.

Crumpton offers a second practice, communal ritual, which is relevant to healing trauma caused by the tormenting touch of a teenage abuser to their intimate partner. Crumpton writes, "Rituals provide a method and practice for bringing the individual and community together to acknowledge the unrecognized traumatic transitions that occur in women's faith lives as a result of childhood [and adolescent] sexual assault, molestation, incest, rape, battering, and other forms of abuse."[4] Referring to womanist care rituals, Crumpton argues for pastoral caregivers to provide ritual spaces with women of all age groups that enhance their "power within community" (the underlying element in personal and institutional encounters that affirm their humanity) and "power within" (the interior sense of agency and value that emerges through intimacy with self and God).[5] These forms of power through communal ritual can beat back "power over" from an abuser. Communal rituals with teenage victims of intimate-partner violence are important for healing from touch that traumatizes.

The challenge for religious leaders regarding physically abusive touching in teen dating relationships is to provide effective pastoral care. This means to give careful attention through observation and listening, "to interpret theologically the cause of suffering and to discern what is needed," and to offer "accompaniment, guidance, and support."[6] These are the fundamental aspects of pastoral care that should be provided to any suffering person, specifically to a teen suffering from physical abuse in a dating relationship. Developing pastoral care skills for all members of a congregation, including teenagers, through observing and listening is essential to good ministry. These skills are helped by knowledge about the physical, mental, emotional, and spiritual developmental aspects of adolescence. Understanding adolescent thinking and brain development as well as the cultural context of an adolescent is foundational to observing and listening. Aspects of adolescent development also inform the theological interpretation of a teen suffering from gender-based violence and inform methods of support for the teen with their parents and teenage perpetrators who inflict violence.

Good pastoral care first depends on a good relationship between the pastor and the teen. Teenagers have a keen sense of authentic care from an adult, specifically a pastor or youth leader. Observing and listening to teenagers helps build good relationships between clergy and teens. A pastor or youth leader should get to know the teens in their congregation, especially those active in the youth group. Knowing their names, their families, who their friends are, and what they care about is the entry point for good relationships. Recall how good it felt when your senior pastor called you by name and knew something about your school activities and your achievements. Showing genuine interest in a teen is the pathway to a teen trusting you during times of crisis. Teenage trust is built on a good relationship with the teen.

Tormented Touch and Race

Mixed-race abusive touching by an teen intimate partner raises concerns about the place of race and racism. As discussed earlier, the history of mixed-race miscegenation laws in the United States and racism collude to complicate matters related to Black and white teens in a violent romantic relationship. Micro-aggressions from the white partner about the Black partner are emotionally abusive. Gina Robinson, a womanist scholar-practitioner, discusses the impact of microaggression on Black Christian girls in the Chicago suburbs in various contexts.[7] Citing Derald Sue and colleagues, Robinson defines microaggressions as "brief and commonplace daily verbal, behavioral, or environmental indignities, whether intentional or unintentional, that communicate hostile, derogatory or negative racial slights and insults toward people of color."[8] Using ethnographic methods, Robinson discovered that girls in her study were most affected by microaggressions that they experienced in suburban schools that affected their identity and Christian formation. While Robinson does not focus on Black girls' experiences of teen dating violence from teenage boys or girls of any race or ethnicity, her work on microaggressions sheds light on how this form of racism can manifest in teen dating relationships. An example would be a white boyfriend telling his Black girlfriend that her kinky hair is abrasive to his hands. Or a white boyfriend telling his Latino boyfriend that he doesn't look Mexican, and that is why the white boyfriend chose him to date. In both instances these are racist microaggressions in a teenage intimate relationship that imply the white race is superior to other ethnic minorities. As discussed above, Crumpton labels such abuse as "power over," which is emotionally abusive.

While microaggressions among mixed-race dating teens should be considered, explicit racial macroaggressions are equally egregious. When one teenage partner hurls racial epithets at their racially/ethnically different partner, the bonds of love and trust are damaged and possibly destroyed. Microaggressions and macroaggressions among mixed-race teen relationships are both racist forms of teen dating violence.

Pastoral Care for Queer Teens

Tormenting of the tangible gift of the teenage body happens among sexual-minority teens in dating relationships. Teens who identify themselves as LGBTQIA experience physical and emotional abuse in dating relationships. The movie *Pariah*, written and directed by Dee Rees, illustrates the importance of pastoral conversations about intimate relationships among queer teenagers and the potential for torment or harm. This movie is a good visual case of teen dating violence at the intersection of not only sexuality but also race, gender, and religion.

Alike, the central character in *Pariah*, is a Black teenage butch lesbian living in Brooklyn, New York, with her parents and younger sister. As this aspect of her identity evolves, she hides it from her sister, who already knows and keeps it a secret; her father, who is unaware; and her mother, Audrey, who believes Alike's best friend, Laura, is influencing her daughter to be a lesbian. Audrey's denial about her daughter's sexuality is fortified by her biblically based religious convictions that same-sex romantic relationships are sinful. In an effort to steer Alike away from Laura, Audrey introduces her daughter to Bina, a teenager who is a member of their church and attends regularly. Alike reluctantly agrees to hang out with Bina after church and school. The teenage girls discover their mutual interest in music and poetry. Audrey is pleased that her daughter is spending more and more time with Bina, a supposedly straight Christian girl, rather than Laura, the sinful lesbian. Alike and Bina's relationship deepens as they spend more and more time together.

During an overnight stay with Bina, Alike gets her first kiss from Bina. Shy and innocent Alike is embarrassed to reveal to Bina that not only was this her first kiss but that she is a virgin. Her trust in Bina assures her that their touching, caressing, and kissing is evidence of their deepening love for each other. The next morning Alike tells Bina how much she enjoyed their intimacy and asks her to go steady. However, Bina tells Alike she is not "*gay* gay" and that their evening of pleasure was all in fun. Bina derides Alike, saying her expectations of their relationship were unwarranted. Alike is emotionally devastated, quickly gathering her belongings and running home in anger and tears. Alike's first experience of intimate touching resulted in emotional torment by someone she trusted and with whom she longed for a loving romantic relationship. Additionally, the emotional torment she suffered was from another youth in her church who mutually agreed to their intimate touching.

Pariah also gives visual insight on the way religious beliefs can torment queer teens who desperately seek clarity on their own sexual and religious identity. Choosing healthy relationships is central to that developmental task. Pastoral care from a religious leader can offer preventative guidance that leads to wholesome relationships when queer teens yearn for dating relationships.

Arthur David Canales, associate professor of pastoral theology and ministry at Martin University, writes:

> Pastoral care is a relationship and it is primarily concerned with human benevolence, empathy, and compassion. Technically, there are no "official" set standards for pastoral care, but some basic competencies for pastoral care are: empowering; liberating; listening; healing; sustaining; guiding; reconciling; and nurturing a person toward God, self, or the other.[9]

Canales offers a checklist for pastoral caregivers of transgender teenagers. While there is no specific reference to teen dating violence among sexual-minority youth, the checklist is helpful to pastoral caregivers in ministry with teens in abusive dating relationships.[10] I have edited the list to be relevant for pastoral care for teens experiencing or at risk for teen dating violence.

- Examine your own assumptions. Assume that
  - Teen dating violence may not be the issue that brings a youth to seek pastoral care.
  - A teen may not wish to explore causes of teen dating violence and/or their sexual identity.

- – Because of social pressures, the stance of the church, and general attitudes about teenage gender-based violence, straight or gay teens may avoid identifying their sexuality or naming an issue of dating violence.
  - – Nothing is surprising about teen dating violence and sexual minorities.
- Be informed about
  - – Advocacy programs, help lines, books, web pages, films, and teaching videos
  - – Pastoral counselors, spiritual directors, psychiatrists, and psychologists who work with teenagers in violent relationships
  - – Doctrines, practices, and policies of your denomination or religious organization regarding teen dating violence or gender-based violence issues
  - – The words and terms that you use describing teen dating violence and sexuality
- Be self-aware of
  - – Your own attitudes and responses, regardless of your own history of gender-based violence and your own sexual orientation
  - – Your own limitations concerning your scope of pastoral care
  - – Your own feelings toward the person receiving your pastoral care
  - – Boundary issues in your pastoral care relationship
- Respect your teenage care-receiver's
  - – Position on gender-based violence, orientation, identity, personal integrity, cultural assumptions, and lifestyle
  - – Privacy by not asking inappropriate medical or psychotherapeutic questions
  - – Personal pain, suffering, and continual struggle with their internal conflicts
  - – Individual capabilities to find their own pastoral solutions

Canales concludes his checklist with the caveat that providing pastoral care to trans adolescents—and, I add, teens in violent dating relationships—may not be easy for those who work with them. "The natural inclination is to give advice, which is not always recommended or needed."[11] However, the checklist helps those who want to provide pastoral care in a manner that empowers teenagers to mature in healthy dating relationships.

Healing Tormented Touch

Pastoral care and counseling with teens in violent relationships must focus on prevention that cares for the teen and intervention that provides healing. Most importantly, a pastor should refer a teen and their parents to a counselor, psychologist, or psychiatrist. "Refer, refer, refer" is what my former colleague, Rev. Paula Dobbs-Wiggins, MD, would reiterate to her pastoral care students. She wanted them to understand the importance of referring traumatized parishioners to psychologists or psychiatrists such as herself, specialists who have far more specialized experience than the average pastor and, more importantly, the licensure to do psychotherapy. She admonished them to notice the signs of abuse and trauma in a person who came to them, and then wisely and quickly refer that person to a specialist. Alice Graham, professional pastoral counselor and retired professor, also stresses the importance of referring as she offers advice on pastoral care for religious leaders as they seek to offer counsel about touching and intervene in gender-based violence among teens.[12]

- Assess your own understanding and experiences of touching. Understand that your counselee has an experience and history of being touched in different ways and may not be able to distinguish a bad touch from a good touch.
- Determine whether the parent should be in the room.
- Encourage the teenager's own sense of power in telling their painful story. For example, instead of hugging them or giving them tissues when they cry, make tissues accessible so they can dry their own tears.

- Be patient and practice deep listening. Never push for details. Allow them to tell you what they can.
- Control emotions and remain calm. Cry or scream after the pastoral care session is over, if needed.
- Focus on questions of context so you can get a frame for what's going on. Ask questions like, "Does your mother know about this? Does your father know about this? Who is this person?" to help you intervene appropriately.
- If the teen presents a danger to themselves or others, or if the teenager is still at risk, then you as a pastor have the duty to report to appropriate authorities.
- Have another trusted person close by for your protection. Teens may attempt to seduce their pastors as a distorted way of getting healing.
- Prepare to refer the teen and their parents to a professional counselor.

Graham continues with other practical advice on pastoral care with teenagers, specifically pastoral conversations about dating and marriage.[13]

- Ask the teen: What do you expect to get out of dating? A pastor should ask this question and listen carefully to what the youth says, because young people have all kinds of fantasies about what dating is going to be. It's important for them to voice their fantasies, just to say these things out loud with a trusted adult who is not there to make a judgment, not there to give them the dos and the don'ts— unless that's called for at some point. Be aware that each teenager is coming from a family system that has certain values that can shape the way a teen thinks about relation- ships and dating.
- Be aware: Young people need to have a safe space to share their thoughts, feelings, and experiences. And they need to be able to hear how things are different for different people in their group, different expectations. Prepare to ask the teen a series of questions.
- Ask the teen: What would you like a date to be about?

- Then ask: How do you want things to be? What is it you're wanting? What do you want your dating to lead to? Talk plain to teenagers. They need clear speech, void of judgment and moralism.
- Ask: What does love feel like? Have your list ready to probe or respond about what love does not feel like, including that love does not hurt.

Care Rituals as Prevention and Intervention

Just as the Eucharist is a powerful ritual for Christian formation of teens, so too are rituals of healing for teens traumatized by intimate-partner violence. Crumpton shares an example of a ritual for healing of women and girls that she observed and participated in at the Afrikan Presbyterian Church in Lithonia, Georgia. The ritual of Eight Bowls is an Afrocentric ritual that can be used in healing for women and girls, enhancing power within the community as well as power within the self.[14] From her observations, Crumpton notes important requirements in preparation for a ritual to heal trauma from touch that torments by a partner.[15]

- Use language that invites participants to engage in the ritual. Clearly communicate the ritual process and expectations. Obtain consent in some form, preferably written, about participation. Stress that it is voluntary.
- Create a safe ritual space for participants to benefit from the experience. Stress the aim of healing aesthetically and not retraumatizing.
- Attend to intragroup dynamics that avoid retraumatizing participants. Consider previous relationships with participants. Build community with all participants before extending invitations for participation.
- Retain someone with clinical experience to participate in the ritual if the facilitator does not have the professional training.

- Attend to self-care for the facilitator. Convening a ritual experience is demanding on the psychological health of the facilitator.

In all instances when providing rituals for healing, Crumpton says that symbols, metaphors, and language should "point toward existential realities that offer new possibilities for meaning making"[16] for a traumatized teen. With Crumpton's suggestions for rituals in mind, below is a ritual for teenagers who have experienced dating violence.

Ritual for Reclaiming Innocence

A ritual for reclaiming innocence intends to restore and enhance the chastity of trust, freedom from violation, and reclaiming of power within for the traumatized teen. When a teenager freely expresses love, care, and commitment to a partner, there is an expectation that their beloved will cherish these precious gifts. However, when emotional or physical abuse hurts the giver of such priceless gifts, their unconditional trust is distorted or destroyed. The practices of giving freely are halted, and their own self-defining power stops. Reclaiming innocence empowers the abused teenager to return to the center of their identity and allows them to trust again.

The Invitation

- In addition to Crumpton's guidelines above, this ritual should aim for similarities among participants, such as gender and sexual orientation, if possible.
- Develop creative ways to build community among participants if it does not already exist.
- Send e-invitations to teenagers, limiting the group to eight or ten persons. Require an e-reply and parental consent. Parents are not invited to attend.
- Invite professional pastoral counselors and psychotherapists to accompany the teens. Be careful to have the appropriate

ratio of teens to professionals. For a group of ten teens, have no more than two adults in addition to the facilitator. Adult facilitators should fully participate in all aspects of the ritual while being attentive to providing care for and counseling the teens when needed.

Materials, Supplies, and Preparation

- Each participant should bring their favorite childhood or baby picture printed or on their cell phone.
- Provide colored and white construction paper, some cut in four-by-eight-inch rectangles; coloring pencils and crayons; Play-Doh; and a keyboard, guitar, or other musical instruments.
- Place a photo printer on a separate table in the room. Provide an iPad or tablet to play back video recordings.
- Prepare an aesthetically colorful yet calming table in the center of the room.
- Play appropriate instrumental music to set the tone for the ritual.

The Process

Direct the group to form concentric circles, with selected adults, including professional counselors and the facilitator, forming the outer circle. Convene the group with words of welcome, stating the purpose of healing for the body, mind, and soul through reclamation.

Invite each teen to bring their childhood or baby picture to the center table, followed by briefly sharing a story about the picture and how they feel about that time in their life. Invite the teens to share their understanding of *innocence* and any other related terms with the group. They may either stand next to the table or return to the circle when they share their story. After all the teens have shared their stories, summarize the themes of innocence from the stories.

Allow the group a few minutes to reflect silently after the summarization, using music as a background. After silent reflection, invite teens to find a partner to talk about what they have heard. Encourage them to share their thoughts on innocence and the meaning of reclaiming their innocence as they are comfortable.

Invite the teens to create new forms of innocence by selecting art supplies, musical instruments, or whatever they need from the table of supplies to re-create an image, poem, or song of reclaimed innocence. Allow time for the teens to create their new images through their art.

Monitor the time needed for each participant to finish their new image of innocence. Afterward, invite everyone back to the concentric circles. Invite adults to bring their new image, poem, song, or music to the table to share with the group. Take a picture of each teen's presentation, to be placed on the table next to the teen's baby image if given permission. The teen may ask the facilitator to use their cell phone to capture their presentation in a video. Transition from one presenter to the next using appropriate words.

The Closing

After the teens have presented their new images of reclaimed innocence, give words of sending forth. Refreshments are appropriate but optional.

Ritual for Parents and Caregivers for Prevention and Intervention

This ritual intends to empower parents and caregivers to be aware of teen dating violence and to think strategically about how to prevent and intervene in abusive romantic relationships of their teens.

The Invitation

- Invite parents and caregivers of no more than ten teenagers. They need not be members of the congregation but must have a connection through their teen's affiliation or membership with the congregation.

- Develop creative ways to build community among participants if it does not already exist.
- Send e-invitations to parents and caregivers. Require an e-reply for attendance.
- Invite professional pastoral counselors and psychotherapists to accompany the parents. Parents may have experienced gender-based violence at some point in their lives. Participation in a ritual on dating violence might trigger unresolved trauma. Adult facilitators should fully participate in all aspects of the ritual while being attentive to providing care and counseling with parents when needed.

Materials, Supplies, and Preparation

- Each participant should bring their favorite picture and/ or artifact of their teenager, from early childhood to teen years, printed or on their cell phone.
- Provide colored and white construction paper, some cut in four-by-eight-inch rectangles, as well as regular and coloring pencils, crayons, and ink pens. Place these supplies on a table near the back of the room.
- Provide envelops and stamps.
- Prepare an aesthetically colorful yet calming table in the center of the room.
- Play appropriate instrumental music to set the tone for the ritual.

The Process

Direct the group to form concentric circles, with selected professionals, including professional counselors and the facilitator, forming the outer circle. Convene the group with words of welcome, stating the purpose of empowering parents and caregivers to be an informed and active presence in their teen's life for the prevention and intervention of teen dating violence.

Invite each parent to bring their picture and/or artifact to the center table, followed by briefly sharing a story about the item(s) and how they feel about that time in their teen's life. Invite the parents to share one word that captures their feelings at this time. They may either stand next to the table or return to the circle when they share their story. After each parent has shared their story, summarize the themes from the stories.

Allow the group a few minutes to reflect silently after the summarization, using music as a background. After silent reflection, invite parents to find a partner to talk about what they have heard. Encourage them to share their thoughts on teen dating violence and the meaning of other relevant terms, such as *repentance* and *care*, as they are comfortable.

Invite parents to write a letter to their teen that includes a promise to protect them from abusive romantic relationships by becoming aware of and taking action against teen dating violence. Encourage creativity such as art, prayers, and poems in the letter.

Monitor the time needed for each participant to finish their letter. Afterward, invite everyone back to the concentric circles. Invite participants to address an envelope to their teen and place a stamp on it for mailing to their teen, to be mailed by the facilitator. Transition from the preparation of the letter to a closing worship.

The Closing

Worship should be short and celebratory, consisting of songs, prayers, and a dismissal.

Notes

1. Rev. Andy Stoker, interview by author, July 13, 2020, Zoom.
2. Stephanie M. Crumpton, *A Womanist Pastoral Theology Against Intimate and Cultural Violence* (Palgrave Macmillan, 2014).

3. Crumpton, *Womanist Pastoral Theology*, 128.
4. Crumpton, *Womanist Pastoral Theology*, 137.
5. Crumpton, *Womanist Pastoral Theology*, 143.
6. Barbara McClure, "Pastoral Care," in *The Wiley-Blackwell Companion to Practical Theology*, ed. Bonnie J. Miller-McLemore (Wiley-Blackwell, 2012), 273.
7. Gina A. S. Robinson, "Educating Black Girls Enduring Microaggressions in an Oreo World," *Religious Education* 118, no. 5 (2023): 459–74, https://doi.org/10.1080/00344087.2023.2268446.
8. Robinson, "Educating Black Girls," 459–60.
9. Arthur David Canales, "Ministry to Transgender Teenagers (Part Two): Providing Pastoral Care, Support, and Advocacy to Trans Youth," *The Journal of Pastoral Care & Counseling* 72, no. 4 (2018): 251–56, https://doi.org/10.1177/1542305018790277.
10. Canales, "Ministry to Transgender Teenagers," 252–53. The text was edited to be appropriate for pastoral care with teens in abusive romantic relationships.
11. Canales, "Ministry to Transgender Teenagers," 253.
12. Alice Graham, interview by author, August 10, 2023. We focused on a number of issues, especially touching on practical ways to help religious professionals prevent and intervene in teen dating violence. Graham is a retired pastoral counselor. She worked some thirty-five years as a pastoral counselor in pastoral counseling centers and had her own center for ten years in northern Virginia. She was on the faculty at Hood Theological Seminary for ten years teaching in the field of pastoral care and counseling. She was also an adjunct teacher at Howard Divinity School and at Wesley Theological Seminary. Graham received her PhD from Northwestern University, where she was the first African American woman to graduate from the joint PhD program at Garrett Evangelical Theological Seminary and Northwestern University in 1983, with her degree in pastoral psychology and counseling.
13. Graham, interview.
14. Crumpton, *Womanist Pastoral Theology*, 138–41.
15. Crumpton, *Womanist Pastoral Theology*, 138–41.
16. Crumpton, *Womanist Pastoral Theology*, 141.

Chapter Five

Advocacy as Theology in Motion

In November 2019, a gregarious star radio host launched a weekend of activities for one of several Hackathons for South Africa: Digital Solutions for Real-World Challenges. The presenters noted the genius of the conception of the program and the high expectations of the participants, who were to develop ways to help people at risk of gender-based violence. I was one of three education consultants among about twenty software developers, business managers, lawyers, accountants, bankers, and financial advisers. No one needed theological advice, although that was also my background, just a sounding board to hear and offer suggestions about their educational conceptual framework.

The Nerd Birds were an all-female group of four Muslim and Christian young women from the University of Cape Town and the University of Stellenbosch. They were creating a video game to teach fourth-grade students about human sexuality. It would include a module about good and bad touch and boundaries, among other modules that would raise students' awareness of power and control and the rights of individuals. The course and curriculum was designed to replace the current public school course that focused on identifying body parts. Most of the groups had educational components for potential users of their products, some more extensive than others.

The first-place winner of the hackathon was Smartware, a group that proposed software that would alert authorities that someone was in danger of a sexual attack by the victim or caring bystander merely shaking their cell phone. The phone would ping a cell phone tower even if the owner didn't have cell phone data, which is costly for a poor South African woman or girl. The second-place winner was the Nerd Birds. The aim of the cash awards was to encourage the groups to continue developing their projects and software. There were several honorable mentions, including M-TeTo, which proposed a program for school-related gender-based violence that included a search engine with regularly updated statistics and suggested guidelines to help faculty address the problem in their school environment. The young software developers at the hackathon embodied hope through advocacy and service to end the tormenting of the tangible grace given to every young person by preventing and intervening in teen gender-based violence.

Theological Definitions of Advocacy

Using Numbers 27:1–8, regarding the daughters of Zelophehad, womanist theologian Delores Williams defines both theology and advocacy. She writes: "Theology, here, means the study of a community's way of talking about God and about God's relation to the world the community inhabits. Advocacy means to talk, write, and/or act in favor of something; it could mean to plead the cause of someone, as lawyers often do."[1] Williams points out three important aspects of Numbers 27:1–8 that illustrate "what can happen when God-talk and advocacy for women come into relations."[2] First, poor women demonstrate the courage to approach the leader or authority to change a law that was historically and culturally shaped in patriarchy. Second, the leaders (Moses in the Numbers text) have the wherewithal to go to God for direction because they realize their leadership will be challenged in a patriarchal society. Third and finally, God advocates on behalf of the daughters of Zelophehad.[3] The theological insight, Williams argues, is that "advocacy by God and man can yield justice for women." Williams maintains that the text must be viewed in its ancient context that "God, through Moses, appears to be effecting systemic change."[4] Thus, the formula for a theology of advocacy appropriate for a religious community is

> Courage to seek justice + Wisdom of a leader to seek God's help through advocacy + God's advocacy = Justice and Advocacy

Williams's observation that here "God [is] imaged as working in the context of patriarchy to advocate" for the right of the daughters of Zelophehad to have economic power is applicable to God's advocacy against the patriarchy that fuels femicide and gender-based violence.[5] Together, patriarchy and power over women and girls' bodies are the lethal combination evidenced in gender-based violence that youth inherit and model. In gender-based violence, patriarchy and power manifest to torment the tangible flesh, minds, and spirits of teens.

A turn to the New Testament reveals another point on advocacy in Scripture. Jesus advocated for those on the margins of society, including children and women. Jesus advocated for the woman caught in adultery in John 8:1–11. The religious leaders, the scribes and Pharisees, brought the woman to Jesus to test his adherence to the law of Moses. They chose the least among them, a woman who had no social or political capital in their day. Jesus, the embodiment of freedom, had the courage to advocate for the woman. He demonstrated justice and advocacy.

Not only is advocacy understood from a biblical perspective but also *kerygma*, or proclamation, which means not only talking, writing, or even acting on behalf of a person or group but also proclaiming on behalf of a person or group. Maria Harris, professor of Christian education, offers this interpretation of the Greek word *kerygma* in her work, identifying five components of youth ministry. She contends that *kerygma* is the ministry of advocacy. "Advocacy is the work of the church in speaking to institutions on behalf of young people, listening to young people, and offering young people opportunities to speak for themselves."[6] Harris draws on Acts 2:42, 44–47 to develop the five forms or central elements of youth ministry, which she identifies as "continuing in the teaching, the *didache*; praying, breaking bread and praising God, or *leiturgia*; being in communion and holding all things in common, or *koinonia*; speaking the word of Christ, of Resurrection, and witness . . . , or *kerygma*; and moving out to those in need, or *diakonia*."[7] Advocacy understood as *kerygma* holds congregations and their pastoral leadership responsible for speaking on behalf of teens to any and all institutions that harm or have the potential to harm young people in mind, body, and spirit. Advocates should confront schools; institutions of employment or work; local, state, and national governmental agencies; and ecclesial institutions on behalf of teenagers. Advocacy of this nature requires those who walk beside youth to listen attentively to their concerns as well as to empower youth to speak for themselves.

Advocacy as *kerygma* calls religious leaders and pastors to be responsible for speaking on behalf of youth to institutions—schools, workplaces, the church—as well as for speaking to institutions about gender-based violence as tormenting the bodies of young people involved in violent romantic relationships. Advocacy as proclamation means speaking on behalf of youth to institutions that turn a blind eye to sexual harassment, incest, and molestation. It means listening to teens and hearing them into speech, or into their own voice speaking their own words. It means allowing teens to speak aloud the physical, emotional, and spiritual pain they experience from gender-based violence.

Advocacy on behalf of teens who experience dating violence requires courage in Christ through the power of encouragement from the Holy Spirit, who is at work in the world today.[8] The Holy Spirit gives power to be courageous advocates.[9] By "courageous advocacy," I mean the resolution or inner conviction to act in spite of obstacles and fear, realizing that action toward justice assures life and flourishing of abused teenagers.[10] While the Holy Spirit experiences the pain and trauma of the sexually abused teen, the indwelling Spirit, who lives in our bodies, also empowers youth pastors and religious leaders to be advocates for teens who are at risk for or experiencing intimate-partner violence. The youth pastor who had a teenage girl experiencing sexual abuse by another member of the youth group, a story I told in chapter 3, not only was struggling with the practical steps of what he should do but was also afraid of the fallout once the parents of the teens knew of the situation. The Holy Spirit encourages youth pastors to act on behalf of the welfare of their teenagers with the confidence that the Holy Spirit will empower them.

Advocacy as Policymaking

There are openings for advocacy not only for religious leaders but also for policymakers and other individuals who are interested in intervening in teen dating violence. For example, state-level policymaking is captured in the National Conference of State Legislatures database, whose primary purpose is to work toward effective state legislatures and to foster cooperation and exchange among states.[11]

The database's definition for teen dating violence, taken from the Centers for Disease Control and Prevention, names violence that "occurs between two people in a close relationship and includes four types of behavior: physical violence, sexual violence, stalking and psychological aggression. [It] can take place in person or electronically, and it affects millions of U.S. teens each year."

By October 2018, twenty state legislatures offered legislation to empower various officials who work with teenagers to prevent or intervene in teen dating violence. The data report captured the various laws that were implemented in those states up to and including legislation in 2014. By contrast, the database captured in August 2023 included a total of eleven states, which indicated a decrease in legislation on teen dating violence on the state level. Beginning in January 2023, California and New York had more policies than all the eleven states.

California has four policies that are in various stages of consideration. The teen dating violence awareness policy, adopted in February 2023, requires recognition of Teen Dating Violence Awareness and Prevention Month in February of every year, with programs and activities that raise awareness about the dynamics of teen dating violence and that support youth in learning skills to have safe and healthy relationships. Sexual health education and HIV prevention education comprise a bill that's pending as of April 2023. The California Healthy Youth Act wishes to require school districts to offer all pupils in grades seven through twelve comprehensive sexual health education and HIV prevention education. While the sexual health education and HIV prevention education is tabled, the teen dating violence prevention education "online information and resources" bill was passed and approved by the governor on July 13, 2023.[12] Legislation about teen dating violence prevention education online requires the state Department of Education to make learning resources available for professionals. Last, there are criminal procedures regarding teen dating violence in ten other states with pending status as of March 2023.

New York has five bills that are at various levels of consideration. Three bills, all of which are pending, focus on school-based teen dating violence programs, which are slightly nuanced to require development of a prevention program, involvement of school districts to create guidelines for implementation of the programs, and incorporation into a school district's existing health curriculum. Comprehensive Sexuality Instruction for Students and State Commission on Intimate Partner Violence are two bills still in debate.

While California and New York have multiple laws for the prevention of teen dating violence, some states introduced only one bill—and even this one bill failed to receive enough votes to pass. Texas had a policy that recommended establishing an Office of Community Violence Intervention within the Department of State Health Services. Florida had four obscure bills that related to prevention of teen dating violence, and all failed to pass. These bills had vague names unrelated to teen dating violence but were categorized as such. They were named Required Instruction in Public Schools, Water Safety, and Required Instruction in the History of Asian Americans (two separate bills with the same name). All the bills on the National Conference of State Legislatures website indicate successes and failures of states to develop and pass legislation for the prevention of violence in youth's romantic relationships.

Teen dating violence policies on the local municipality or city level are not evident. Further research is needed to determine whether there are teen dating violence policies on the local municipality level. Reviewing the National Conference of State Legislatures website suggests that several policies are specific to local school districts. It's safe to assume that policies on the state level govern the local city governments.

Advocacy as Church Policy

Policies also can be developed on the church or judicatory levels, regardless of the denomination or affiliation of a congregation. From the local congregation level all the way up to the judicatory level or national and international levels, policymaking is necessary. Consider the case of domestic violence awareness that took shape in the Christian Methodist Episcopal Church as an example of policy development in a denomination. The process and experience of the Christian Methodist Episcopal Church is a case study for how congregations can work from the local level up to the highest policymaking body of their religious institution, not only to encourage speaking about the nature and prevention of domestic violence but also to encourage congregations to shape policy related to teen dating violence. The Christian Methodist Episcopal policy, paragraph 554, "Domestic Violence Awareness policy," sets a precedent for future policies that can be specific to teen dating violence. It also serves as an example for other religious institutions and individual churches to follow.

Advocacy Through Partnerships

A variety of partnerships can be developed between schools and local authorities such as police, social workers, health care professionals, and especially those organizations involved in teen dating violence prevention work. Partnerships with court officials, juvenile court judges, and court advocates can likewise alleviate the problem. Michelle April Benjamin, a family lawyer and judge in the Cape Town law courts, grew up in a household in which her mother was severely abused by her stepfather. Benjamin has developed programs to work with youth living in shelters and who have experienced dating violence. She has found it important to have initiatives and best practices that help people in general—but youth in particular—to become aware and involved in preventing teen dating violence.

Benjamin started the Let's Talk movement to help girls not only become aware of gender-based violence but also identify or find themselves in Christ as a way of nurturing their spirituality. She hosts an event every year where girls meet to talk about the issue of gender-based violence. She has learned the importance of being tolerant of and patient with young people, and of parents being aware of how their behavior at home influences their children—not just their violent behavior but also in general how they carry themselves and interact with others. She emphasizes Psalm 139, which speaks of being fearfully and wonderfully made, as being foundational for her own ministry.

Other partnerships are possible when considering organizations concerned about nurturing healthy teenagers. Be strategic about partnerships to reach local and regional audiences especially during Teen Dating Violence Month in February, Women's Month in March, and Domestic Violence Month in October. Consider the following:

- Partner with the Boy Scouts, Girl Scouts, Boys and Girls Clubs, and other youth-serving organizations to develop strategies to lobby local and state governments about the prevention of and intervention in teen dating violence.
- Partner with schools to include curriculum on teen dating violence in the appropriate junior and senior high school curricula.
- Partner with national nonprofits to promote awareness of teen dating violence on their various media platforms. Such organizations include Southern Black Girls and Women's Consortium, Love Our Girls, and college and alumni chapters of sororities and fraternities.
- Partner with ecumenical and interfaith organizations that have gender units. The World Council of Churches addresses gender-based violence primarily through the Just Community of Women and Men unit, specifically its Thursdays in Black international program.
- Develop partnerships for writing grant proposals to fund agencies that welcome prevention of and intervention in teen dating violence

Advocacy Through Practice

A final way of doing advocacy is to practice being an advocate. By this I mean looking for and being aware of teen dating violence and then advocating with and for teens.

Try practicing advocacy with congregants who are concerned about teen dating violence—and with those who are not yet aware of it or are resisting stepping in to prevent it, perhaps because they don't know how.

- Use case studies to analyze, identify, and focus on the problem of teen dating violence.
- Use *Theater of the Oppressed* lab exercises and role-play as ways to embody strategies for identifying and acting against teen dating violence.[13]
- Practice advocacy techniques with teenagers in violent relationships.
- Develop a local hotline in your church, or partner with other churches and a youth-focused institution to develop a hotline.
- Produce podcasts about teenage gender-based violence.
- Provide help information in women and men's bathroom stalls in churches that is easy to get and privately carry (business card–size information).
- Use social media to raise awareness about teen dating violence.

Use of Case Studies

Below are two sample case studies that clergy and church leaders can use as practical exercises to develop their approaches for advocacy. To use them as practical tools, first read the case study and then discuss the questions, which are designed to help participants practice doing advocacy work.

A Case Study: Troy "Likes" Tonya

Shortly after he started sixth grade, 12-year-old Troy told all of his friends how much he liked the new girl at their school, Tonya, and he boasted that soon she would be his girlfriend.[14] Troy spent a lot of time following Tonya around school, and he made sure he sat next to her in every class they had in common.

When she would walk by him, he would stare at her and make comments about her body, which became increasingly sexually suggestive, especially if he was in the company of his friends. For her part, Tonya tried ignoring Troy and, on several occasions, including in the presence of his friends, she told him to "Stop it," and to "Shut up," but he just laughed and taunted her more. When he started touching her, she complained to her teachers and she also told her parents. School officials said they would talk to Troy, but he remained undeterred. One day, in front of his friends, he came up behind her and began rubbing his genitals against her buttocks while explicitly asking her for sex.

Tonya, who up to this point had always been a good student, started missing school and her grades dropped dramatically. Her worried parents noticed that she wasn't eating and that she was spending most of her time in her room, isolating herself from family and friends. Tonya's parents' alarm grew when they found what appeared to be a suicide note written by Tonya. They acted quickly to get her counseling, but they also filed a criminal complaint against Troy as well as a federal civil rights lawsuit against the school district. The grounds for the civil suit rested on the argument that school officials were aware of Troy's behavior but did little to stop it, thereby violating Tonya's civil rights. The court agreed with Tonya and her parents, emphasizing that the behavior of her male classmate was not "bullying," but rather sexual harassment, which is a violation of Title IX of the 1972 Education Amendments Act. By not responding appropriately, the court ruled that school officials had created a hostile and abusive learning environment, thus limiting Tonya's ability to fully participate in, and benefit from school.

Possible questions to discuss:

- What's going on in the case that merits addressing teen gender-based violence? What is the situation? Make a list of your concerns to determine the priorities.

- What are some possible ways to address the problem, particularly as it relates to advocacy? Who should be a partner?
- What information is needed? What would the police need to know about the situation? The social worker? The judge? The state legislator?
- What resources are needed? Financial? Temporary protective care?

Case Study: Dad's Last Love Note

This case study provides an opportunity to consider advocacy about teen dating violence after a teenager has been stalked and murdered by an ex-boyfriend.[15] While based on an actual event, the storyline and characters are fictional.

> Lynzy, my love.
>
> I hope your first day in twelfth-grade year is a beautiful one. I am excited with you. My beautiful baby girl is a senior in high school!
>
> Love ya,
>
> Dad

I would put them in her backpack, in places where she would not miss them. When she got her first cell phone, I texted my beautiful daughter love notes. We shared a special bond, as she was the oldest of my two children and only daughter.

In January 2015, the second semester of her junior year, Lynzy started to date a guy who lived a few miles away from our home. His name was Jason, and he was a senior at a different high school from Lynzy's beloved Bally Senior High. I never really understood why she was attracted to him. He was rather plain-looking and quiet, very different from her previous boyfriend. She never really talked about why she was interested in him. I didn't know why I didn't like Jason. I just didn't, and I never said anything to Lynzy that would cause her alarm. It was just my fatherly intuition, and I had no basis for alarm—until she mentioned that he would send her text messages all through the day asking her what she was doing. Once she said he was never interested in meeting her friends. She even decided not to attend her junior prom because Jason said he didn't like dancing. I thought what a very shy fellow he was but never stopped to wonder about his behavior.

Around June, when Lynzy started to work as a lifeguard at the local swimming pool, she met Jeff, another lifeguard. She started chatting about Jeff so much, how they had common interests, that I wondered whether she would soon break up with Jason. Well, it happened. One day after work, she and Jeff went to get pizza. Jason saw her with Jeff. When he publicly confronted her about being with another guy, she decided to break things off with Jason. She told me all the ugly details of Jason accosting her, but I didn't offer her any advice. I didn't really know what to say. I just listened.

Lynzy did break up with Jason and started dating Jeff just as the summer was ending and school started back. She was so excited about her last year in high school, prom, graduation, and going off to college. Occasionally she mentioned Jason's attempts to get back together, but she refused him.

On December 15, just before Christmas break, Jason called Lynzy and asked her to go out to return items they had given to each other when they were dating. Lynzy agreed to meet Jason on December 21. At that time, I didn't know they were going to meet. I was working an extra shift at the power plant. My wife, Lenora, told me Lynzy was going out with Jason that night and that she was happy he would soon be out of her life completely. I sent Lynzy a love text filled with kiss and hug emojis. That was the last love note I sent her.

Lenora called me around one a.m., worried about Lynzy being late. Lynzy had said she would be home by midnight. I sent her a text message, "Hey Babygirl, what's up?" but didn't get a reply. Moments later, I received a phone call from the police that I should come immediately to Main Street Pizza Parlor. After telling my supervisor I had an emergency, I left for the pizza parlor. When I got there, I saw the police car and ambulance in front. I knew my Lynzy was dead. It was the same pizza parlor where Jason had confronted her when she was with Jeff.

I left the scene and went to the police station. I didn't know what I was supposed to do. I drove home to tell my wife and son that Lynzy was not coming home. Her ex-boyfriend had murdered our Lynzy.

Days of shock and pain turned into months and then two years after my Lynzy's death and burial. Jason was arrested for first-degree murder, tried in the city courthouse, and sent to prison with a life sentence. My wife, son, and I have attended counseling since our daughter's death. I've started my own teen dating violence intervention program. I named it "Dear Lynzy" to commemorate the love notes I once sent her and the series of letters I began writing to my daughter after her death. Writing the letters in my journal brings me comfort. I talk to high school students about how they might avoid violent dating relationships. I also talk to parents about teen dating violence.

> Dear Lynzy,
>
> I am standing in room S-205, the room you were in as a high school senior. I'm talking to the students about dating violence. Yesterday, I talked to some students at the high school where Jason attended. God, I hope I can help just one girl or boy from being abused, or worse yet, murdered. I am not sure how long I will keep this up. I'm doing it to honor you.
>
> Love ya,
>
> Dad

Possible questions to discuss:

- What were the signs of abuse that the father should have identified in his daughter's dating relationship?

- How could he have responded? How could his wife, Lenora, have responded?
- What ways could Leonard and Lenora partner with Lynzy's high school?
- What ways beside lecturing to students could Leonard be more convincing regarding teen dating violence?
- What opportunities does Leonard have with other parents to help prevent and intervene in teen dating violence? What opportunities for advocacy do they have?

Case Study: Developing Denominational Policy

During Domestic Violence Awareness Month in 2009, the Ministers' Spouses of the Dallas/Fort Worth Region of the Christian Methodist Episcopal Church held a workshop for local women and men. Rev. David Isom, a senior clergyperson in a California Christian Methodist Episcopal congregation and a professional social worker, presented statistics about gender-based violence in the area, noting a young woman who was killed by her husband a few days prior to the workshop. The young woman was a member of a church located just a few miles from where the workshop was being held. A clergywoman stated that the slain women was her sorority sister, saying that it was reported—and police evidence proved—that, fearing for her life, she had previously asked for police protection from her abusive partner. The recognition that the victim had cried out for help to members of her congregation and the police sparked the testimonies of other women in the audience. Six women talked about how they had been beaten, strangled, or even shot by their spouses.

Members, including me, helped to draft a resolution for the Christian Methodist Episcopal Church on domestic violence for consideration at the denomination's General Conference. After producing several drafts, we did indeed submit our resolution for consideration at the 2010 Christian Methodist Episcopal Church General Conference. It took eight years of repeatedly teaching and lobbying local and regional churches about the need for a policy on gender-based violence before the General Conference approved it in 2018. The policy was added to the Christian Methodist Episcopal Church Discipline. It is paragraph 554, "Domestic Violence Awareness," and it reads:

> Each local church is encouraged to establish a Domestic Violence Awareness Ministry; and/or partner with a local Domestic Violence Shelter/Program in order to create awareness, education, direct services, prevention and crisis intervention programs with a focus on helping to address the needs of those individuals and families who are victims or survivors of domestic violence within their local church. Pastors and ministers will speak out and send a message that domestic violence is unacceptable under any circumstances, and is contrary to the biblical teachings; they will offer hope, healing, patience and understanding.

Possible questions to discuss:

- What is your local church or denomination's policy on domestic violence? Is it relevant to teen dating violence?
- What are the steps for proposals or resolutions for new policies?
- Which religious leaders—bishops, general secretaries, women, youth, young adult groups—will support and promote the need for policies for the prevention of and intervention in teen dating violence?
- How is the implementation of new policies monitored on local, regional, and international levels in your church or denomination

Working with State and Local Governments

It is important to contact state legislators about teen dating violence concerns and the need for legislation. Here are some suggestions for religious leaders to advocate for policies on the state level:

- Inquire about what possible policies are and who is available to introduce the legislation you think is needed.
- Push your state congressperson(s) to introduce the policies you think are needed to help prevent teen dating violence.
- Develop a relationship with state congresspersons whom you trust.

Additional Practices

Here are two possible practices that churches or congregations can take on. First, have mandatory classes for youth on sexual health, HIV prevention, and teen dating violence prevention. If possible, integrate these types of programs into the overall programs for youth and young adults rather than making them special or one-off events. The Christian Methodist Episcopal Church considers youth to encompass those age twelve to seventeen, and young adults to encompass those age eighteen to thirty-five. It would be appropriate to propose and pass legislation requiring such classes for these particular age groups and to note that in the denominational body of law.

Second, observe Teen Dating Violence Month, which is February in the United States. This observance became a national policy under the Family Violence Prevention and Services Act.

Notes

1. Delores S. Williams, "A Theology of Advocacy for Women," *Church & Society* 91, no. 2 (November 2000): 4–8.
2. Williams, "Theology of Advocacy," 5.
3. Williams, "Theology of Advocacy," 6.
4. Williams, "Theology of Advocacy," 6.
5. Williams, "Theology of Advocacy," 7.
6. C. Dykstra, "Portrait of Youth Ministry," *Religious Education* 76, no. 6 (1981): 674–76.
7. Maria Harris, *Portrait of Youth Ministry* (Paulist Press, 1981), 13.
8. Karen Baler-Fletcher, *Dancing with God: The Trinity from a Womanist Perspective* (Chalice, 2006), 19.
9. Evelyn L. Parker, *Between Sisters: Emancipatory Hope Out of Tragic Relationships* (Cascade Books, 2017), 106.

10. My definition of courageous advocacy is influenced by Rev. Dr. Martin Luther King Jr.'s contrast of courage with cowardice in *Strength to Love* (Fortress, 1963), 122.

11. "About Us," National Conference of State Legislatures, https://www.ncsl.org/about-us.

12. California Legislative Information, July 13, 2023, https://leginfo.legislature.ca.gov/faces/billNavClient.xhtml?bill_id=202320240AB1071.

13. Augusto Boal, *Theatre of the Oppressed* (Theatre Communications Group, 1985).

14. This case study has been adopted from Cindy L. Miller-Perrin, Robin D. Perrin, and Claire Renzetti, "Abuse in Adolescent and Emerging Adult Relationships: Peer Sexual Harassment, Sexual Assault, Dating Violence, and Stalking," in *Violence and Maltreatment in Intimate Relationships* (Sage, 2018), 172–73.

15. "Dad's Last Love Note" is based on the case study "'Dear Lisa': Murder by an Ex-boyfriend," in *Teen Dating Violence: The Invisible Peril*, by Susan M. Sanders (Peter Lang, 2007), 13–17.

Index